EYES WIDE
OPEN

A FIRST-TIMER'S GUIDE TO THE REAL WORLD OF
BOARDS AND COMPANY DIRECTORSHIP

ROBYN WEATHERLEY

First published in 2015 by Major Street Publishing Pty Ltd
Contact: info@majorstreet.com.au or ph: +61 421 707 983
© Robyn Weatherley 2015
The moral rights of the author have been asserted

National Library of Australia Cataloguing-in-Publication data:
Creator: Weatherley, Robyn, author.
Title: Eyes wide open: a first-timer's guide to the real world of boards and company directorship/Robyn Weatherley.
ISBN: 9780994256003 (hardback)
Notes: Includes index.
Subjects: Boards of directors.
          Directors of corporations.
          Corporate governance.
Dewey Number: 658.422

Cover design by T.ANJI (contact: mylucky.25@gmail.com)
Internal design by Production Works
Printed in China by Asia Pacific Offset Limited
10 9 8 7 6 5 4 3 2 1
ISBN: 978-0-9942560-0-3

Disclaimer and small print

The content of this book comes from the life experience and education of the author, culminating in many years of corporate governance experience and hundreds of hours spent around Australian boardroom tables with every type of company director.

The personal insights shared by the author represent her own opinion solely. If anyone believes they have featured somewhere in the content it will be due to co-incidence or an honest recognition of their own behaviours (good, bad or otherwise). The book has been sensitively written so as not to identify anyone by name or any other characteristic which could make them obviously recognisable to the public.

The fact that an incident, experience or personal reflection has been included is because the author has seen it with her own eyes – at least once but possibly more often – and it's quite likely she's seen it across more than one board or industry.

Where the author has shared the ideas or work of others, this has been acknowledged in the text and further reference of the source has been included where possible.

Praise for *Eyes Wide Open*

"I have had the pleasure of observing Robyn in action and working with her a few times over the last eight years. She has also taken the minutes of some board meetings I have chaired. Robyn is a consummate professional. She has used her extensive knowledge of governance and secretarial matters from inside numerous boardrooms of substantial organisations to produce a very comprehensive and insightful book that is full of wisdom and practical advice. This book is a must-read for first-timers and those wanting to learn more about the important intricacies and nuances of becoming a great company director."

NICHOLAS S. BARNETT
Chairman & corporate governance expert,
Chairman – Ansvar Insurance and Director of Mission Australia.

"The first taste of life's great experiences is always memorable, but seldom the best. Experience usually pays for itself, many times over. Many of my adult friends have often lusted after and propelled themselves into their first board directorship, only to discover a bitter taste in the mouth later because they have stepped in where angels fear to tread. Women especially have been blindsided about the reality of becoming a director because, until recently, that professional career has been secret men's business.

"Robyn Weatherly's book *Eyes Wide Open* is an excellent resource for aspiring directors with little or no experience that can be used to test themselves on the hard facts of board life, what they need to know before consent is given, and also the complex relationships they must manage. Finding a board is a significant piece of detective work. There is hard data and also actual personalities and key relationships to be researched up front and these are often available only from the outside looking in. Even when you have been made an offer, the smarter detective candidates complete their final validations before they grant consent. Arriving at the board table –the new director's behaviour, questions and relationships all need to be managed in distinct and professional ways. The reader will find all these stages and challenges well analysed by Robyn, together with research points, issues and data to be probed before that final clinch is embraced! And no matter how excited you might get.

"Looking back on my own twenty-five years' experience on public and private boards, I have found Robyn's advice and suggestions to be right on the money. In fact, I wished that I had this book to read when I was starting out. There are many boards out there with no sense of direction, no fear of flying and a willingness to bank you and your reputation into their own mostly futile attempts to cash out an unknown future. Don't get caught amongst their number.

"Read Robyn's *Eyes Wide Open*, so yours are. Keep this book close by in your early years as a director and you will undoubtedly make more successful choices and not find yourself having just boarded the next disaster express."

PETER WILSON AM
Chairman of AHRI Ltd and Yarra Valley Water

"In *Eyes Wide Open*, Robyn Weatherley sets out to de-mystify the topic of how boards work and what company directors actually do. And she succeeds brilliantly! This book is written in a conversational style, packed with practical advice and real anecdotes that shine a light into the boardroom in a unique way which informs, explains, amuses and enlightens. If you have ever thought you might like to become a company director, this book is for you!'"

ANNE WARD
Chairman Zoos Victoria, Colonial First State, Qantas Superannuation, CIE;
Director, MYOB, Flexigroup Ltd, Foundation for Imaging Research Council;
Member Advisory Council, RMIT

"As the author notes – 'Don't be overwhelmed… just be proactive, educated and informed' this is exactly what *Eyes Wide Open* does from a unique perspective. I thoroughly enjoyed being part of a conversation, just like catching up with a friend over coffee, hearing about the ins and outs, dos and don'ts of directorships. A must-read for aspiring directors and those relatively new to the boardroom and as such, is now part of the curriculum for 'Pathway to Your Potential' program for directors."

DR JESS MURPHY
Founder of Pathway to Your Potential programs and
Director of Outside-In Business Advisory Services Pty Ltd

"I wish this book had been available before I joined my first board. It provides fantastic insight into the working mechanisms of the board, the challenges and opportunities, and what you need to do to be an effective director. A must-read for every first-time board director."

MICHELLE GIBBINGS
Founder and Director, Change Meridian

For Dottie, Steve and Rupert

CONTENTS

FOREWORD BY THE HON. STEVE BRACKS AC

IT IS NOT often that you gain an insight into the company boardroom. How it works. What it means to be a non-executive director and why key relationships do matter.

But that is just what Robyn Weatherley's timely book does. It is a well-written, insightful account from an insider.

It avoids the textbook account of a directorship and rather offers the inherently human account in an engaging conversation with the reader.

It also adds to the debate on the diversity and expertise now required for effective, well-functioning boards. The hints and tips related to behaviours, etiquette and key relationships are also telling.

There is a significant commitment and diligence required for a board director to be effective.

This is captured effectively throughout the book.

Eyes Wide Open is a must-read for busy executives and managers who may not have had the opportunity to see inside a company board. They will be better informed and equipped as a result.

The Hon. Steve Bracks AC
Former Premier, Victoria, 1999 to 2007
Chair Cbus Superannuation Fund
Chair AFL Sports Ready

WHY THIS BOOK IS DIFFERENT

WHEN THE IDEA to write this book first came to me, I felt driven and totally committed to its realisation. I knew I had something of value to share from a unique standpoint which could really make a difference to the experience of people contemplating directorship, becoming directors for the very first time or wanting to be a more insightful director.

I felt that if I could share my many years' of corporate governance experience, working so closely with boards, perhaps new and aspiring directors could take on their roles and responsibilities with their eyes wide open – regardless of what type of company the appointment would be with – be it a small not-for-profit, an equal representation board, government enterprise, tech start-up, or an ASX-listed company.

It is important to me that I share my knowledge as a *conversation.* I want this book to be interesting and engaging so that you enjoy reading it as well as learning from it.

The insights I want to share come from the undeniable privilege I've enjoyed sitting at a great variety of board tables for many hundreds of hours and from being around directors and in board environments for many years, learning from and observing some of the very best practitioners in the country. Of course, I have also observed their distant cousins and no-one's favourites, the less-than-average directors.

Directorship in Australia is a vastly populated club. There are literally thousands of individuals actively overseeing the operations, governance and strategies of every sort of company, commercial and government enterprise. There are just as many variations of people in that group as you could ever imagine – all with different personalities, coming from different backgrounds with varying degrees of commitment. Unfortunately, as the statistics tell us, there are also far too few women on the vast majority of boards. It is a significant and urgently overdue commercial imperative for our governments, companies, networks and the directorship community to address collectively. It's no secret that drawing the talent required for our boardroom tables from just one half of the population is ludicrous – think of the qualities and experience going to waste in the 50% not being considered for such roles. That's before you get to the research which confirms the financial returns accruing to companies that have higher female representation on their boards. Women and all forms of diversity around a boardroom table is simply good for business – period.

In terms of director types, there are those who are professional directors – they hold multiple appointments in their portfolio and it's their full-time job; they generally commence their journey either at the end of a hugely successful commercial or professional career, or they start to transition while still holding down a super-busy executive or professional role. These directors may sit across very high-profile boards, a smattering of the ASX-300 company boards, but also sometimes there will be one or more not-for-profits (NFPs) or government board positions thrown into the mix. Their boards may preside over entities worth many billions of dollars and therefore some of the country's largest employers, taxpayers and community contributors. They bring to the table their extensive skill-sets, including though not limited to: commercial; project; entrepreneurial; regulatory and governance experience; and a deep commitment to directorship – so many of Australia's exemplary directors are in this category.

Others on this path find themselves introduced to board opportunities as a result of the constitutional or shareholder rights their employer or an associated body has with a particular company (industry super funds with equal representation boards can be examples of this). The nominating associations are very closely aligned with the interests of the company's members (as they are also *their* members) and so, on account of this affiliation, the directors on these boards are often said to 'have skin in the game'.

The governance and corporate communities are also now starting to see the impact and rising profile of much younger directors creating and leading their own companies – those under 30 have been making their mark across many sectors of the economy and on a variety of boards. Often as the founder of the enterprise, these young people may find themselves as the managing director or the chairman of the board either very early on in their career, or indeed as their first appointment. These directors are typically highly entrepreneurial and have sometimes been involved in commerce or not-for-profits in some very dynamic way since their teens. They bring a confidence, youthful perspective, energy and drive to a boardroom that is sometimes overlooked (and badly needed) when board compositions are being reviewed or due to be refreshed. Younger directors should be well regarded in the composition mix, given their generally strong understanding of social media, the adaptive cultures of young people and because they can represent that population demographic which companies are often striving to reach out to.

Then you have NFP boards, which can be magnets for directors seeking their first-time board experience, usually driven by the cause concerned and the exciting and sincere opportunity to contribute to something they believe in. People very gladly and diligently give their time and contribute to these companies, sometimes for many years on a totally unpaid basis. At the other end of the spectrum, you also find the highly experienced 'who's who' of Australia's directors, with impeccable credentials, serving not-for-profit boards, bringing with them considerable networks, industry connectivity, commercial experience and sometimes strong philanthropic attributes.

I could go on and on here. There are the directors who sit on the boards of family companies (which can be everything from small enterprises to very large, multi-faceted, international or complex groups); those who run associations and clubs; and those appointed to government boards. There's a smorgasbord in Australia of companies and entities for people to consider when seeking a board appointment, depending on where they are at on their directorship journey and where they'd like to go.

Despite this variety of boards, however, it doesn't mean it's all fair game when you start looking for appointment opportunities. Ensuring you are properly positioned with the relevant skill-sets, have adequate time to commit to the task and are an appropriate fit for an appointment is absolutely critical. I talk later about the incredibly serious side to being a director which, regardless of the board you join (as far as size, type, complexity, balance sheet strength is concerned) will neither diminish nor wane – not even for one minute of any day, of any week, month or year during your tenure.

Directorship is a wonderful privilege bestowed by society on those who willingly put their hand up to say '...I will knowingly put my assets and reputation on the line for the betterment of this company and those it serves'.

WHO AM I TO BE GIVING OUT THE ADVICE?

I LOOK TO my experience as a story to be shared with others who find themselves in this new and bizarre, tribal territory called the 'boardroom'.

I've worked with everyone from deeply experienced directors, to those who are board-ready and seeking their very first appointment, and I know exactly what their concerns, fears and unknowns are. Unless you've actually been in a boardroom and sat through an entire meeting (and more than one at that – in fact an entire year of meetings) it's difficult to really know about the 'ins and outs' beyond the texts and journals you can read or what you see in a TV drama series. What you don't see or read about are the situational and professional matters and details that go hand-in-hand with directorship (both at and away from the board table) and which no-one really tells you about upfront. If you had a sneaky insight into just some of these things going in, you might feel that little bit more match-ready when fronting up for your first game.

It's like joining a new animal herd (don't be offended – you'll appreciate the analogy I'm trying to draw here). As a brand new director, or someone going onto a board for the first time, you need to see yourself as something akin to a little elephant who is newly birthed into a long-established and well-populated herd which, by its nature, has its own cliques, territories, systems, culture, codes of communication and conduct already established – all of which are known and adhered to (or at least understood) by the current group.

As the brand new baby of the herd you can avoid getting your little toes stepped on by the bigger bulls and cows by getting some inside tips from another worldly elephant in the group. Makes sense, doesn't it? Limping around in the corporate jungles of Australian boardrooms with a big sore elephant toe can be avoided and I'll tell you how you can achieve this.

My insights can't save you on the courtroom witness stand if you neglect your legal obligations and duties as a director (that's of your own doing); however they might just allay some insecurities or uneasiness on the occasion of your very first appointment, or when you are moving up the director ranks into larger commercial enterprises and suddenly you are working with professional secretariats and a whole new level of boardroom sophistication and complexity.

I've had the fortunate experience of being privy to the board tables of a multi-billion dollar ASX-listed entity, a massive industry super fund, medical companies, an insurance company and other variations of operating collectives. My university and post-graduate education spreads across business[1], legal and governance areas[2], I've published through the AICD *Company Director* magazine[3], on LinkedIn and I was a founding member of National Australia Bank's extraordinary Board Ready program.

Board Ready was started a few years ago by myself and some beloved NAB colleagues. It was developed from nothing but our own education, experience and a burning drive to teach women how to be first-time directors – giving them a direct insight into how it actually works through demonstration, education and collegial support. This series

[1] Bachelor of International Business, Griffith University Queensland 1993
[2] Master of Applied Law, University of Queensland 2006
[3] "Visiting the Frontline", *Company Directors* magazine, Australian Institute of Company Directors, July 2014; http://www.companydirectors.com.au/Director-Resource-Centre/Publications/Company-Director-magazine/2014-back-editions/July/Opinion-Visiting-the-frontline; (member only access)

has propelled many women at NAB onto their very first board and has connected them with new and valuable networks. Importantly however, it gave them the confidence to put their hands up and get inside that room. Breaking down the expectations, responsibilities and also the pragmatic matters that go with directorship was an incredibly important part of the program. We wanted to give these women something more than they could get from a textbook.

It's all very well giving you tonnes of theory but if you've never been at a real-life board meeting, what you really need is an inside view on how it actually works in practice.

If I wasn't a director at these board tables, then what was I?

Sometimes my role has been as a company secretary or lead corporate governance adviser to a board or committee or group of committees. Sometimes I was charged with the integration and management of governance capabilities and services across an organisation and that meant attending every board and board committee meeting held by that company (in parallel to being there in a governance advisory capacity). Other times saw me sitting at the table as a contractor running my own business as a governance adviser and minute-taker. In every case, regardless of what my formal role-title was, I have been the minute-taker. Someone has to do it and while it means spending many more hundreds of hours typing out the board's minutes and re-living a variety of discussions, in my opinion it's one of the best gigs you can get in a corporate career. It's also the only one that allows you to share in, or be privy to, the company or board's glory for all the great decisions made; you are also in the fortunate position of being able to duck and run when the bad ones come home to roost (unless of course you've been part of the debacle for some reason).

Sitting in my chair I get a ticket to the grandest game in corporate Australia, i.e. the opportunity to sit around the board tables of some of our most exciting, progressive and interesting companies, observing how companies develop, grow and contribute to the economy; watching and learning from some of the sharpest, most commercially-experienced and exciting minds in the country. I also get to see how people react and respond to very difficult, pressing and uncertain times. In my role, I have been privy to some of the most amazing information sessions, presentations, decisions and discussion experiences, and that's what always makes it worth the admission price.

Attending meetings with some of the most highly-regarded and experienced directors in Australia during the global financial crisis, for example, was undeniably one of the greatest educational periods of my career. What I saw and learned during that period, on a professional level, can't be taught at university, learned through director tutorials or read about in a textbook. Observing these directors as I did, managing their way through exceedingly difficult and complex decision-making (as was the case for a great deal of institutions at the time) was both uplifting (to see how they lived with, carried and extinguished that degree of responsibility) and scary at the same time (given what was at stake for the economy). I hold those directors and executives in the absolute highest regard for their courage, tenacity, leadership and ability to remain steady in the face of immense difficulty and uncertainty.

Boards need directors with big shoulders to make big decisions that can sometimes directly and significantly impact the financial and economic health of our economy.

To be in the company of those directors and to observe their conduct during the GFC was a definitive educational and career privilege.

That's not to say that I also haven't been privy to decisions taken by the boards of smaller or different companies which have been just as impactful on the lives or commercial outlook of many of their shareholders and stakeholders.

Companies don't need to be behemoths for their decisions to be any less scary or of a lesser consequence for those who will live with the outcomes of those decisions.

Being around boards and directors every day of my career is what has set me up to share the valuable advice and hints that you find in this book. It's not only what happens inside a boardroom during a pre-set agenda that counts, it's all the administration, volume, regulations, planning, execution, co-ordination, relationships, diplomacy and meeting expectations that happen outside the boardroom that add up to the great story and marvellous education that I share with those who are intrigued by the inner workings of this space.

So I get the pressure. I get the importance of how these things can and do play out. I get the depth and complexity of matters you have to consider and that you are on the hook for them all the time. The responsibilities and decision-making don't ever go away; the work doesn't get any easier or less voluminous. I understand your frustrations, the unrelenting pages of papers to read in your board pack (as it's usually me who has compiled and sent you these meeting packs, so I already know what's coming your way).

> *I understand your ambition for your company and your stakeholders. I get how much hard work goes into being a director. I do, because I see it every day. It's all I do.*

The insights I want to share may make you feel a little more comfortable in your role, just a little sooner, freeing you up to concentrate on the bigger matters at hand, i.e. helping your board to build a strong and robust company culture, develop the company's strategic leadership and capabilities and create and grow its financial strength and long-term sustainability.

An exceptional director

What I've compiled in this book are some attributes and insights which I hope will help, in a small but meaningful way, to make you an exceptional director. In my opinion, being an exceptional director is quite frankly what every director in this country should be aiming to be when they sign their Consent to Act. If that's not your intention, you should do the company and society a favour and find something else to do. Because being an exceptional director should be a non-negotiable in this game.

Society gives companies a licence to exist through its laws and governance systems. Society also grants people the opportunity to sit on boards and to partake in the privilege of leading our companies. Your appointment necessitates and demands an exemplary contribution to the corporation, because it is society – and therefore all of us – that suffers from the unfortunate incompetence of under-committed and under-educated business leaders including those at the board table.

Let's be frank, if you really stuff it up you can find yourself on the front page of the *Australian Financial Review*, or on the TV news as you walk into court with a legion of lawyers and their voluminous team of juniors who you personally can't afford, or who are costing your shareholders or members an arm and a leg, on the charge of not having fulfilled your duties and obligations as a director. You could wear a very large financial penalty that your company may be prohibited from insuring you against.

Then there's your reputation at stake too which in the small corporate world that is Australia cannot be re-built easily or a fresh one bought off the shelf. Bad stuff can happen (to both the good and the not so good) and it's a daily risk for any director.

Directors who are fully committed to their roles are acutely aware of their obligations and responsibilities, and acknowledge the relentless (though sometimes enjoyable) ongoing education required to stay up to date with advancements in governance, risk, strategy, the law and financial best-practice. These are the directors we must support, nourish, guide and advance through our commercial enterprises and governance systems. These are the people who have an exceptionally reduced chance of being seen on the court-house steps.

Confidence in the key

My experience means that I can confidently step into any sized boardroom, of any company or industry type, and deal with any level of director present – and it is this confidence I want you to have. Don't ever forget that regardless of who you find yourself sitting next to, at the end of the day, they are just a person – someone who eats, drinks and functions exactly the same way as you do. As I sometimes say to colleagues or junior staff who are intimidated by their company's chair or any one director (having met them or not), they all put their pants on one leg at a time just like the rest of us. Don't lose sight of that, and don't be overwhelmed by the résumé of anyone you find yourself sitting next to. Use it as an amazing opportunity to learn, listen, absorb and advance. Enjoy the ride and the gift of the discussions.

All great directors start from somewhere (everyone has to have a 'first' appointment, a first meeting, ask their first question, etc.), and most people feel slightly overwhelmed, unsure, unsettled or just excitedly nervous (or a combination of all of the above) about taking their first seat at the board table. Everyone comes from a starting block somewhere – you all just end up swimming down different lanes of the same pool.

In *Eyes Wide Open* I will share things with you that may not come to your attention via traditional means. I'm not out to offer a prescription for perfect success as a director, nor do I hold that my view is the only one that counts. However, insider-tips and advice from someone in the know never goes astray when you are venturing into new fields. Researching the composition of your first or next board takes on just the same importance. I'll talk to this further in the book.

Generally, the majority of publications, courses, journals and articles produced for aspiring, new or developing directors focus heavily on the legal obligations and responsibilities, duties and educational basics expected (and rightly so). However, rarely does anyone sit you down and tell you how to navigate your way through this experience (behaviourally and culturally) from one particular side of the fence – the company secretary's side – and how knowing about some very small or minor points upfront could make your directorship experience just that little bit grander, less opaque and more fulfilling more quickly.

So what doesn't this book do?

Good question…before we get started, just to be clear – this book will not and was not intended to:

1. Educate you extensively or completely in your legal director's obligations and duties and how to discharge them (although I do give you an overview in the form of lists and referencing for you to do more follow-up work)

2. Teach you how to be financially literate – that's for your own separate education and ongoing development (although I do talk financials in Chapter 2)

3. Tell you how to negotiate director remuneration (including how much – if any – to expect and how it should be paid)

4. Give you any short-cuts of any kind, which – should you implement them – would mean you could skimp on, or do anything less than a stellar job of being a director.

Item 1 is to be garnered through your own private study and by maintaining a contemporary understanding of the directorship landscape. Pre- and post-appointment, this is your undertaking until the day you hand in your last board resignation.

Item 2 is an imperative for you to conquer, or at least reach a certain level of proficiency in, prior to any appointment (I'll go into this in much more detail later).

Item 3 is beyond the scope of this book and totally out of my professional realm – it's a speciality all of its own.

Item 4 just isn't my thing. If you haven't noticed already, I hold all directors to a very high bar, so don't think I'm going to be leading you down short-cut paths at any point.

Also, I'm making an assumption that the company you are joining is neither a pass-through entity nor a dormant one, such that your directorship is merely a formality of law or other. No, I'm assuming that the company your board sits across is a proper, functioning, operating entity.

Before we move on to the chapters, take the time right now to pause and really think about WHY it is you want to be a director. WHY is it that you want to sign up to the time, legal and societal obligations, not to mention the reputational and financial risk that is irrevocably assigned to directorship.

You know, you may not actually 'get' it until you've been on a board for some time. Even people who are long-time executives and who have spent years in their commercial roles working with boards can't believe the difference it means being on the other side of the table.

You have to be patient in slowly building up your knowledge and experience-base as a director because you didn't become a CEO, engineer, executive or the head of a retail juggernaut overnight and neither will you become competent in this role immediately. In your day job, you incrementally built your experience and skills which led you to larger, more senior and more complex opportunities. It's the same thing with directorship. It's a game of building-blocks, learning incrementally and taking in everything you can to elevate yourself into that special group of directors that sits at the apex of boards in Australia – the exemplary directors. If we put on our honesty hats, these are the ones who senior management, your shareholders, stakeholders, regulators and the secretariat really want at the board table.

Some books can be read in any order, chapter-wise, but can I ask you to do one thing for this book?

Please **read the whole thing**.

It's only because the conversation really takes hold once you've got *all* the insights. Otherwise, it's going to be a bit more piecemeal for you, which won't be nearly as satisfactory and complete as reading the whole book.

It's not a big book so make sure you get to every part.

Let's get into it then.

PART ONE

PRE-APPOINTMENT

Don't underestimate the benefits that will
accrue to both you and the organisation from
undertaking the following pre-appointment
steps – thoroughly and seriously.

1

WHERE TO BEGIN

A WHOLE LOT of pain can be easily avoided by nominee directors who take the requisite steps and time to understand exactly what it is they are signing up for and getting into – **before** signing the Consent to Act.[4]

Being asked to join a board or nominate for a board appointment is usually a big deal for most people and can reflect very long-held ambitions. Those who've been there before understand and appreciate the reality of the time, commitment and tremendous upside (and risk) that come with these opportunities. However, there are a number of things that you need to both consider and become comfortable with before you say, "…where do I sign?"

"There are no secrets to success. It is the result of preparation, hard work, and learning from failure."
Colin Powell[5]

---

[4] Section 201D *(Corporations Act 2001)* www.austlii.edu.au/cgi-bin/sinodisp/au/legis/cth/consol_act/ca2001172/s201d.html?stem=0&synonyms=0&query=consent%20to%20act; accessed 22nd March 2015

[5] www.brainyquote.com/quotes/authors/c/colin_powell.html; accessed 23rd March 2015

In the first part of this book, I deal with the initial research points that you need to take care of. We take a snoop around the internet and make sure your intuition is happy for you to proceed to the next base. I'll step you through some related categories, each with its own checklist, so that at the applicable time, you can cross-check the homework that you've done against that which is recommended you do as a minimum.

A caveat here is that the extent and timing of each stage of your due diligence will vary depending on the types of companies you are considering. In saying that, there are minimal non-negotiable steps that I recommend you take when joining ANY company, even those at the smaller end of town. That is because the regulators, the law and our society set baseline expectations for directors of all companies regardless of their status.

So at the appropriate time in the following discussion, I'll point out when you should be stepping up your pre-appointment enquiries. But let's get through the common-to-everyone checkpoints first.

Check the core alignment

At the very heart of a company or organisation is an underlying cause, business, set of values, mission statement or reason for being that got the whole thing going in the first place. Before you join the board, examine what that is, make sure you understand it and can support or defend it.

In joining a board you will need to satisfy yourself that you truly support the actual nature of what it is the company does and what your role on the board will be (this is particularly so for very small companies where it can be all-hands-on-deck for directors). If you are looking at a very small board that's steeped in charitable work or some other public good, as part of the gig you can sometimes (but not always) be expected to fund-raise or contribute money, time or other resources to the company's events or other needs, or find donors or philanthropic support. If that's not your cup of tea, then give those boards that are open about these expectations a miss.

The cause or the business has to come first.

It will be a long and arduous road seeing out a decent directorship tenure if you simply can't stomach the bottom-line reason for the existence of the business itself. No-one needs a board directorship on their CV that much. Your ego must run a clear last in determining your fitness for the appointment. This issue goes beyond being asked to join the board of an organisation that would look amazing on your résumé, but which – if you were being honest with yourself – doesn't really ring your bell (nor ever will) in any shape or form, other than it being in front of you as a directorship opportunity.

You must also ask yourself: are the business's operations, strategies, functions and corporate social responsibility motives and beliefs aligned to your own personal moral compass and ethics? Your name, reputation and potentially your future ability to secure more board positions, or even other executive or commercial roles, could be seriously propelled or (alternatively) significantly stalled by this opportunity sitting in front of you.

Think carefully about how comfortable you will be telling anyone and everyone you come across that this is your board.

If you are still feeling a surge of enthusiasm and delight at this point, then read on.

However, if you are substantially less than 100% convinced, even at this very early stage, dig deep beyond your ego and consider getting off this bus and letting someone else get on who is more aligned to, and comfortable with, what this organisation is and what it does. While some might judge me for this challenge that I'm putting out to you, believe me it's going to be a far easier (and more enjoyable) prospect to see out your director's tenure if your heart is in the company from the start – don't fabricate your enthusiasm for it just because it's a directorship dangling in front of you.

Research, research, research

It's boring, I know, but trust me your initial research into the board position you are considering will be worth it and you'll never have regrets having done it.

Where do you start? Google will be your friend here. Jump online and get a feel for the company or organisation in detail. Look at their website, their competitors' websites, check out their key public policies (check those in the areas of governance, risk, public matters, environmental, social and governance (ESG), political positioning and so on). Get a feel for who they are and what they are.

☑ **CHECKLIST**

☐ Have you even heard of this company before?

☐ Have you ever seen this company on the front page of the newspaper?

☐ To the extent possible via the internet, can you identify the company's reason for existence (who are they, what do they do?), values, mission statement or culture? How does that sit with you?

☐ Does anything at this early stage indicate that they might not align with your moral compass and ethics?

☐ Would you be happy to tell anyone you know that this is your board?

☐ Are you still keen?

If you answered the last question on the checklist in the affirmative, let's keep going.

The board's composition

Before any discussions are held with anyone inside the company (the chairman, CEO or others) you must undertake a good check online (as best as you can from information available) across the board's current composition and the executive group:

- Who is on the board?

- Who are the company's executives?

- How long have the directors been appointed for?

- Does it look as if there's been a lot of turnover, i.e. how many of them have been appointed in the past 12 months relative to the total number of directors on the board? (You can find information regarding changes to the board's composition and shareholders from a 'Current and Historical Extract' which can be obtained online from the ASIC website www.asic.gov.au or from the company's annual report.)

- How diverse is the board (in terms of male/female, experience, education, skills, specialisations, age and where they are situated geographically)?

- When considering their diversity, how does that sit with you?

- Are the directors located (geographically) away from the company's head office or main operating locations?

- Is the board one that follows an equal representation model, or does it comprise a majority of (or all) independents? If it's a family company, who in the family has been appointed and is the hierarchy apparent, i.e. fathers, mothers, siblings, etc. Do they have any other external parties on the board outside family?

- Does it say how directors are appointed, by whom and when? This could give you an important insight into the company's internal processes, governance structures or shareholder influence which in turn might open up further questions to be asked when you meet with the chairman.

- Look at the board's size – does it appear to be a very large board and if so why? You may need to do some further digging on this one with your chairman or your nominating party. If the board is very small and the operations of the company are apparently fairly large or complex, how does that work in practice? The question goes both ways.

The message here is: take an objective and independent lens to the board's size and composition – what's it telling you? Does anything jump out or seem peculiar?

Is bigger better?

Let me drift a bit for a moment. Note that a board is not necessarily sized in proportion to how large the company's operations are. There are two aspects to size. On the one hand, maintaining largish boards (and by this I mean perhaps more than 10 or 12 directors) naturally results in a larger administrative load and cost accruing to the company and its shareholders and sometimes its members. Also, having a larger composition does not necessarily guarantee a one-for-one additive in intellectual capability or workload contribution being returned to the company and its shareholders. In other words, more bums on seats and brains at the table does not mean that a larger board will automatically win the capability race, or guarantee it an enhanced commercial edge over its smaller cousins. Larger boards can be more difficult to move around geographically to visit the company's operations, meet with staff or shareholders, undertake roadshows, etc.

For the less committed and seriously time-poor director, a large board can enhance their opportunity to make smaller and less impactful contributions to meetings and key decisions, and to take more frequent absences from meetings. A big board unfortunately works well for this type of appointee. The chairman presiding over a very large board will need to be highly skilled and experienced and will be continually tested by these elements.

However, there's also the other side to this story. I've encountered sizable boards which have worked surprisingly well and which demonstrate that a larger beast can be just as nimble, decisive and effective as the little whippets. These boards have demonstrated that when (1) the composition is proactively managed, (2) directors are engaged and committed to their cause, (3) the secretariat is ably resourced and authorised to make enabling decisions, and (4) each director has a unique and strong contribution to make (and they follow through on this throughout their tenure) then a larger board can work.

Larger boards are also able to utilise their directors across a multitude of board committees, thus ensuring a fair division of the board's workload.

What's ultimately important is that the shareholders and the board truly believe and can defend the compelling value-add and financial return that comes to the company and its shareholders/stakeholders from having a lot of people on that particular board.

If allowed by its constitution, the current size of a board could also be linked to a succession plan that's been invoked by the company, whereby some longer-tenured directors nearing retirement have agreed to stay on for a period of time to allow newly-appointed folk to get acquainted in their roles before the longer-term directors depart (reducing the size back to something more appropriate or traditional for that particular entity).

The board's size is an issue that's squarely tied to the individual circumstances of the organisation concerned. It may be something that needs to be fully understood by speaking to someone on the inside of the company (beyond what you read on the internet or in the newspapers). So tread carefully and respectfully when making your enquiries or offering up a quick (judgmental) opinion on this topic.

At the other end of the spectrum is a board that is too small and suffers from insufficient resources and a limited capability and time-commitment from its directors. It can work both ways. A board that's insufficiently sized can suffer from lack of diversity of thought, skills and experience, and may not be capable of fulfilling the company's potential. Also, smaller numbers (particularly when close to the quorum minimum) can be inefficient if it's difficult to convene meetings due to the continual clash of diaries (i.e. there's little to no fat between the minimum number required to hold meetings and voting quorums, and the number of directors appointed in total). This can be particularly so if the board is composed of directors who hold very busy day jobs or who must travel a lot for their private professions.

Take account of the size of the board and if it appears quite large (or equally under-done) in composition then make sure this is a point of discussion on your checklist when you meet the chairman.

☑ **CHECKLIST**

☐ Based on the above discussion, what is your feel from the board's composition?

☐ What are your takeaway questions for the chairman, CEO and company secretary in this regard?

Why has this opportunity come about?

There is a reason that a position on the board has become vacant and you need to find this out. You can satisfy your curiosity by answering these questions:

- **Did someone resign?** If yes, why? The answer could open up a whole raft of issues for you to flag on high alert. On the other hand, someone might have been struggling to manage their overall time-portfolio and needed to offload some commitments. Otherwise it could just be that they are moving interstate or overseas, or their tenure has met the company's policy cap and they have long planned to leave the board.

- **Is the board expanding?** If so, why? What's driving the expansion?

- **Is the board diversifying its skills and experience base?** If yes, is that because it needs to in order to deliver on its strategies, remain competitive, or to give it an inside edge on key capabilities that are currently absent? Boards which acknowledge that they need an extended experience-base or skills-set are giving a great clue that they are forward-looking, strategic and seeking to welcome new directors into the fold to strengthen and advance the business. Typically, this should be a sign of a healthy outward-looking and progressive board, which is always a massive bonus!

- **Has the company been taken over (or for government entities, has a new political party been elected) and is the parent (or newly elected PM, Premier or Cabinet) now doing a refresh of appointments?** If yes, what was the background to the takeover and what is the status quo (and future expectations) regarding board composition?

- **Has someone died?** It happens.

- **Is the board in turmoil and can't keep its directors?** If it is the board of a listed company, this will be more easily researched. However, if it is a private company then some sleuth-like, though sensitive, questioning could be in order:

  - Is it just one or two directors causing the pain, or is it commercially- or legally-related, i.e. has it been driven by a dispute?
  - Is the chairman a total lunatic or control freak who does not engender their board's support or respect?
  - What's driving the turmoil and turnover?

  Take care if leaping onto a board that's in distress or is in a vortex. If there's a whiff of trouble in the air, has it been in only very recent times, or is there a long and arduous history to the discontent? Boards are like all good marriages – none are ever 100% smooth-sailing and occasionally they can hit disruptive, unexpected or sometimes fatal bumps in the road.

  At the worst end of the spectrum, the issue driving the turmoil or disruption could be an ugly, deep and costly barrel of nothing-good-at-all, so put on your diving mask and get to the bottom of it quickly though respectfully with your chairman. If the chairman in turn gives you a fairly sanitised or vanilla version of events then the CEO, other directors, the company secretary or the resigned directors are those to make secondary enquiries with (having full and proper regard and sensitivity to the stage of your nomination and the appointment process, as well as the ability or otherwise of the parties concerned to share with you sufficient details on what's gone down).

- **Does the board need to fulfil a publicly-committed diversity quota** (regardless of what type)? If yes, are they seeking the right people for the role, or will anyone with a pulse do (without offence to you or anyone else)? Do query this with the chairman – don't be a token appointment just because the company is looking to meet a public policy or internal commitment of achieving a certain type of diversity by a pre-ordained timeframe to keep their stakeholders happy or to meet annual reporting season expectations. The bottom line message here is be sure that your appointment is valid and supported by the board for the right reasons. On the other hand, if this is a company you'd die to be on the board of and you can live with the tokenism, go your hardest! Eyes wide open, remember?

- **Is the board looking for directors who have strong business or fundraising connections,** or who can be heavily philanthropic towards the underlying charity or business (be it via cash, network introductions, connections, etc.)? This is a must-ask for anyone considering joining a charity or not-for-profit entity, or enterprises that struggle to maintain viable and commercially-sourced revenue bases. It costs nothing to ask the question.

Appointing people who have strong commercial connections or who are networked to others with big wallets is not distasteful or disrespectful per se, as quite often it is the private links and networks of individuals that can really make a major difference to the advancement and growth of our charities and not-for-profit enterprises. The message is to be alert to the prospect if you are heading towards a charitable entity or limited liability public company operating for a beneficial purpose or public good.

Don't forget that charitable and not-for-profit entities benefit from many types of donations, including your time, perhaps your donated resources (non-monetary), your drive, commitment of other skills and even perhaps social media support. It's not always about money but it's a question you should be comfortable to ask early in your due diligence.

- **Final thought: how was the vacancy brought to your attention?** Did you respond to an advertisement, were you approached by a head-hunter, or were you nominated in some other way (by a colleague, peer or mentor, or by way of your role in a sponsoring organisation related to the membership)?

   If you were nominated by reason of your organisational title or position, you are no less encouraged to do every bit of due diligence that any other person would do should they be considered for an appointment on an arms-length basis. Your nominating organisation will not, and cannot, save you from the law or your own reputation if things go wrong on this board.

Be sure you are comfortable with the reasons given for any or all of the above before going too far down the appointment path. If you're told it's confidential as to why the vacancy has arisen, then I'd be pressing for more details or would seek feedback from the chairman, current directors or the CEO (and don't forget immediate past directors, should they be able to share these details with you). Let your intuition guide you here, as this is your very first taste of this board and if you have doubts at this point, it's an opportunity to slow things down and research some more.

Quite simply, if the noise of doubt and uncertainty in your own head gets louder and louder as you progress through the pre-appointment process, there is no disgrace in bailing early and graciously. Don't get wrapped up in the fact that someone's chosen or nominated you for the appointment as the over-arching reason to accept the opportunity. Never feel indebted to any party to voluntarily take on a troublesome role that you could well do without. While it's incredibly flattering in every case to be selected or nominated for a board appointment, once you sign that Consent to Act, you are responsible for your own actions and the actions of the board.

Some people may see it as a challenge or an undeniably magnetic opportunity to join the board of a company that has reasonably-sized or significant problems, irrespective of what those issues might be (e.g. financial, market share, a tainted reputation, etc.). Not all directors, for whatever reason, seek a heavily sanitised appointment.

Understanding and testing your own risk appetite for a board appointment is a fundamental element of your considerations.

✓ CHECKLIST

- ☐ Why has this opportunity come about? What has driven the recruitment?
- ☐ Do you feel comfortable with the answers given to your questions or what you've been able to find out?
- ☐ How was the opportunity introduced to you?
- ☐ What is your intuition telling you?

Everyone's path to appointment will have both commonalities and differences. As stated earlier, it comes down to how and why you were nominated and what the company's internal processes are for appointments. Take each case as it comes and take yourself through the due diligence process step by step until you reach an overwhelming or informed conclusion to go one way or another.

2

COMPANY CULTURE, STRATEGY AND FINANCIALS

*"A business that makes nothing but money
is a poor business."*

HENRY FORD[6]

IF YOUR INITIAL research into the board and its company or business has not put you off, you now need to dig a little deeper. Recall here, that you are still in the infancy of your due diligence and most probably have yet to meet the chairman, CEO, company secretary or other directors.

The board may not have even received or be aware of your application yet, (be it via a sponsor or shareholder organisation, through the nomination committee or via the chairman's or someone else's personal recommendation). Or you could be at the stage where your interest in joining the board is known to others, or your name has been put forward to the director group and is still being contemplated.

---

[6] www.brainyquote.com/quotes/quotes/h/henryford104352.html; accessed 23rd March 2015

Any which way, you are happy enough with what you know about the company at this stage and you could attend a meeting with the chairman, CEO or company secretary with sufficient knowledge to hand and questions to ask to present as a somewhat researched and inquisitive candidate.

Don't forget that this is an interview process for both sides – it is as much about them investigating you, as it is you checking them out.

But there is more work to do before you sign on the dotted line and the following areas should be important components of your deliberations.

The board and the company's culture

This is a big topic and I can't oversell the importance of it enough to you. In all of your research and all subsequent discussions with the chairman or CEO, if you *never* hear the word 'culture', consider running as fast as you can to the door and exit the building. Seriously.

What is culture?

Edgar Schein, an esteemed academic contributor to the field of organisational development and culture defines culture as follows:

> *"Culture can be thought of as the foundation of the social order that we live in and of the rules we abide by…the culture of a group can be defined as a pattern of shared basis assumptions learned by a group as it solved its problems of external adaptation and internal integration, …and therefore to be taught to new members as the correct way to perceive, think and feel in relation to those problems".[7]*

---

[7] https://books.google.com.au/books?hl=en&lr=&id=kZH6AwTwZV8C&oi=fnd&pg=PR9&dq=edgar +schein+culture+definition&ots=9nc2qIBsOi&sig=0nWc1F5IcppCaetmtrn5IbAUOck#v=onepage&q =edgar%20schein%20culture%20definition&f=false; accessed 23rd March 2015

The Investopedia website[8] also gives the following definition of culture:

> It is "...the beliefs and behaviours that determine how a company's employees and management interact and handle outside business transactions. Often, corporate culture is implied, not expressly defined, and develops organically over time from the cumulative traits of the people the company hires...Google's corporate culture has helped it to consistently earn a high ranking on Fortune magazine's list of "100 Best Companies to Work For."

There are too many great companies out there with really good cultures that are more deserving of your time and the risk you are taking to join the board, than to waste it on a corporation that seriously lacks this requisite commitment.

Culture can never be under-done and there are volumes of studies to back this up (just think about your own commercial or professional experience on this point). You can 'buy' a lot of things in the market to support a company's performance (tools, systems, people, etc.), but having a deeply embedded and authentic culture that is owned and valued by every member of the organisation (from the receptionist to the chairman) will get you home every time. This can't be bought off the shelf anywhere, it has to come from the top down and run the full length of the company; it has to be something that exists within the bones of the organisation and it starts with the board. I've only touched on culture briefly here but will go into detail at a much deeper level later in the book when it comes time for you to meet the 'players'.

Don't be mistaken, a company and its board can be many things, but they will never reach their highest potential nor be the very best corporate citizen they can without a strong, robust and authentic culture.

---

8   www.investopedia.com/terms/c/corporate-culture.asp; accessed 18th Jan 2015

☑ **CHECKLIST**

What you are looking for here is not just to read and hear the word 'culture'. You want to learn:

- ☐ How the company and the board lead culture on a daily basis
- ☐ What are the behaviours that are organic to the company and its operations?
- ☐ How is culture tested, how often and by whom? Does this seem sufficient to you?
- ☐ What is the staff turnover like?
- ☐ How does the board work together at meetings and outside of the boardroom?
- ☐ What are the respect levels among the directors for each other, regardless of their backgrounds or appointment circumstances?
- ☐ Behaviourally, what's absolutely never tolerated?
- ☐ Who sets the boundaries of what's an acceptable culture – is culture being led and exampled by the board and the CEO, or is it being controlled or overly influenced by disparate sectors within the corporation?

Culture should be way up high on your list of due diligence questions and, at the applicable time, you'll need to test it with at least the chairman and CEO. If you get a massive variation between these parties, then that's an interesting element for further discussion prior to your appointment or to keep in the back of your mind. Also look for the discussion on culture to be natural, rather than orchestrated, stilted or scripted. This should be a topic of pride for the board and the CEO to speak of (on behalf of management and the company) so your assessment of the culture must naturally figure prominently in the weighting of your due diligence.

"Culture eats strategy for breakfast every time."
Peter Drucker[9]

The strategy, corporate structure, operations and business plan

There's little I need to say to convince you I'm sure as to why obtaining some details on the strategy, corporate structure, operations and business plan is really important to your pre-appointment process. Understanding and getting behind these components (at least some of them) will give you an undeniable edge before commencing on the board. The issue will be just how close you can get to the details before your appointment.

Our friend 'context' will come and go throughout the book – and so it arises here. Getting details on the company's strategy, structure and the business plan (or outlook) will depend on the type of board you are joining and at what nomination stage you are at. It also depends on how much information is available publicly about the company.

I'd hesitate to sign the Consent to Act without a clear understanding and picture of these elements. I'm not saying that you need to categorically be all over and totally conversant with each and every part of these items before appointment (this builds over the time of your tenure) but what you do need is sufficient information on these elements to build your confidence in the company and the board.

You may be able to uncover this information on strategy, etc., prior to signing your Consent to Act, or parts of it may come afterwards. You may be afforded a session with key internal executives who can take you through these matters before your first board meeting but sometimes this comes after you sign your Consent to Act.

It's more than having a bit of knowledge to get you through your first meeting; it's about ensuring you have an informed view of where

---

[9]   Attributed to Peter Drucker; http://en.wikipedia.org/wiki/Peter_Drucker; accessed 28th March 2015

the company's been and where it's going, and it will help you under-stand the inter-connection of these elements with the company's culture and financial position. I talk to these issues in further detail later in the book so we'll definitely return to these points.

Be sure to chew the fat on these topics with both your chairman and CEO (and other executives as appropriate) to a point where you have sufficient information to proceed.

The financials

YES!!! I hear you shout – she finally got there! Don't you go straight to the financials first? Well, no. And you'll notice I've put financials down-stream from culture, strategy, business plan and board composition.

Don't get me wrong, this can and should be one of your BIG deal-breakers (refer earlier note about your personal risk appetite). If there's trouble afoot here, then why did I make you go through all of the other stuff first? There's good reason for this…

Don't be blinded by the financial strength of the company to predominantly justify and pre-empt your decision to join this board.

A financially strong balance sheet and healthy profit and loss (P&L) should not be the only characteristics that tip you over into accepting the appointment – but they sure do help!

Financial positions of companies can change very quickly depend-ing on who's at the helm, the strength, flexibility and robustness of the strategy and business plan, dynamics of the market and the global economy, etc. It will be the company's culture, human capital capabilities, leadership and its change-agility (amongst other things) that will substantially help drive the company through and out of hairy times.

While a very large balance sheet and strong P&L are fabulous starting points to take your appointment forward, don't be totally seduced by these and believe that the rest will take care of itself.

Your ability to get a copy of financial statements will depend on whether the company is public or on the board's internal appointment or nomination processes; this can also determine the timing of when you get to review the financials. Unless the company is listed and/or the financials are publicly available on the internet, you will be asked to sign confidentiality clauses before you are provided with this information (this is normal procedure, so expect it – refer also to the broader discussion on confidentiality agreements in Chapter 3). Some companies may want you to sit and go through the financials with the CFO rather than emailing them to you.

Pre-appointment, definitely get a hold of the financials. Go as far back as you feel you need to go (if you can get five years or more then grab them, but otherwise don't settle for just this year's and last's, because the tale of trends is a powerful one – both positive and negative).

Take a good long look at the financials and see what they tell you.

Your confidence in reading, interpreting and understanding the financials will depend on your experience and financial literacy. If you are fairly experienced and astute at reading financials, but still can't quite work out parts of what's been provided, then ensure that part of your residual due diligence (before signing the Consent) includes meeting with the CFO to work through what you feel uncomfortable about or need clarification on. You absolutely need to understand and get your head around what's going on with the numbers before diving in.

If the industry is particularly complex, multi-jurisdictional or has had a history of difficult financial conditions, be extra diligent in this step and take the time you need to work through anything that's bothersome or that you don't quite understand.

> **WARNING:** *If you can't read the financials, i.e. you don't understand what it is you are reading because your level of financial literacy doesn't allow you to – then don't sign the Consent to Act. You are not ready for this appointment or perhaps any appointment at this time.*

If you are comfortable with what you see (relative to what you know about the company's financials and your own risk appetite), and the records and notes appear clear, informative and in line with what you know about the company's size and the industry, etc., then that's one more box you can tick off.

Financial ratios

Check key financial ratios – ones that you know are imperative for success in this type of industry. How will you know this if the industry is new to you? If you are not a financial expert or accountant yourself, take this up with the CFO, your own accountant (or one at your work) or you can always Google it. There are books aplenty, and heaps of articles and resources online which can help you to understand why particular ratios are important to particular industries. Obviously, the way an industry trades and does business will inherently reflect what makes a ratio applicable or otherwise.

You may also take guidance from the company's CFO, your own director-networks or mentors on which ratios you need an insight into. Examples of standard or common ratios include:

- Current ratio (current assets minus current liabilities)
- Quick ratio (current assets minus inventory, divided by current liabilities)
- Days receivable/payable/inventories ratios
- EBIT (earnings before interest and tax)

- Interest cover ratio (EBIT divided by interest expense)
- Debt to equity, and debt to assets ratios
- Gross and net profit margins
- Returns on equity and assets.

If you detect any deteriorating or other significant trends in any one of these ratios, then always be sure to raise it with the CEO or CFO so that you can understand what's going on behind the scenes. There could be a very good reason for why it's showing up and it may not necessarily have any long-term effect.

Context is everything in reviewing ratios – context re the industry, business type, sources of funding, 'norms', what's best practice, etc. A ratio which comes from industry (x) may well be significantly different if the result comes from industry (y). Not only will this analysis provide you with a solid foundation for understanding the company's past, it will also set you up to comprehend the company's future prospects.

Sometimes the financials will provide you with ratio positions across key result areas and so you may not need to do the calculations yourself, which is always a bonus!

> **TIP:** *Be sure also to review the notes to the accounts very carefully. Going through this detail is important as it may reveal a bunch of information and insights you'd not previously considered or encountered in your main read of the accounts. These notes form part of the financials and so form part of the board's approval of the accounts.*

How does the bottom line seem to you?

Which brings us to *insolvency*. Most people contemplating director-ship in Australia today would understand that the law does not look too kindly upon companies which trade on an insolvent basis. The *Corporations Act 2001*[10] holds that a director has a positive duty to prevent insolvent trading (s588G). What that means in practice is that if the company enters into a transaction that does or would make the company insolvent, and a director is aware (or a reasonable person would be aware) of this at the time of the transaction, then they are likely to have breached the *Act* and may be penalised or disqualified by ASIC.

There are various defences to the charge and it's not the place of this book to go through those details with you (there's a bucket of case law that sits behind this topic). The point of the story is that it's imperative that you be really satisfied with the company's and/or corporate group's solvency *prior* to appointment (this is regardless of your financial or general risk appetite in joining a board). Be really sure and comfortable with this one, as if things go downhill quickly that's not necessarily an experience you want under your belt.

If you are unsure of how the cash flows work, or if you think there could be off-balance-sheet liabilities lurking where you can't see them, arrange an appointment with the CFO and go through the financials. Get all the background and history to anything that you don't understand. Going into your board appointment fully comfortable with the financials is a big plus.

Personal obligations to be aware of going into an appointment

As part of your discussion with the CFO regarding the financial position of the company, ensure they take you through when and how the company pays its employee PAYG contributions, general taxes and superannuation guarantee payments.[11]

---

[10] The *Corporations Act 2001* – http://www.austlii.edu.au/cgi-bin/sinodisp/au/legis/cth/consol_act/ca2001172/index.html#s588g; accessed 22nd March 2015

[11] http://sladen.com.au/news/2013/9/10/directors-liability-for-unpaid-superannuation; accessed 22nd March 2015; article written 10th Sept 2013

Also ask them what the current status is of these payments. You must be confident that everything is in order, as you don't want to find yourself served with a Director Penalty Notice down the track for unpaid taxes or super by the company. Non-payments of these obligations can carry personal liability for directors under qualifying circumstances, so don't overlook checking out these details.

Financial literacy – how well do you cut it?

Now is a good juncture to consider how 'match fit' you are in this area of expertise. There will be many parts of the business, industry or company's products that you can learn about and get up to speed on quickly, both pre- and post-appointment (this is par for the course for all directors joining new boards, regardless of their prior experience).

However, there are no excuses for joining a board without having a decent foundation in financial literacy. It doesn't matter who you are or how amazing the opportunity is. In fact, you are far better off delaying your first appointment until you can undertake some study or upskill in this area to get your skills developed to a decent level – there are risks attached to being under-cooked here.

If I still haven't convinced you, research the Centro case. Google it. Learn from it.

If you are undertaking financial literacy studies you will absolutely come across the Centro case as it's now cemented in Australia's corporate governance history, and provides a mass of learnings for directors, boards, management, legal counsels and company secretaries. You don't need to be on the board of a mega company to be caught up in a similar situation, so take your time to understand the context of this case and what it means for you as a director. It's a disservice to yourself, your board, the shareholders and the community if you join a board without having an appropriate level of financial literacy. This is one responsibility that can't be outsourced or put off until a later date.

If you do not have the required level of financial literacy (and by this I mean relative to the size and complexity of the company you are joining – or wish to join) then:

1. Get yourself educated! Jump online, or on the phone to the team at the Australian Institute of Company Directors (AICD www.companydirectors.com.au) or the Australian Institute of Management (AIM www.aim.com.au) and sort through up-coming opportunities to do some courses in this area. If you are starting at zero, consider whether you will learn more effectively from an online course or if you'd prefer in-class, facilitated learning.

   If you are a director on the board of a superannuation fund, also check out the Australian Institute of Superannuation Trustees (AIST) and Association of Superannuation Funds of Australia (ASFA) sites – www.aist.com.au and www.superannuation.asn.au – for great training opportunities.

   Financial literacy is developed like building blocks – you start from the ground up, one building block at a time. Be sure to choose a course that will suit your own circumstances and experience, as taking on a course that is too complex too soon might cause you to panic or put you off financials generally – and that's not going to help your directorship career as ultimately there's no getting away from balance sheets and P&Ls.

2. If you've been in or around the operation of companies as part of your own business or professional life, then you are probably further down the competency track than a lot of people. However, still take the time to really go through each component of the financials and ensure that things stack up as you would expect them to. Even if you have accumulated some terrific knowledge around financials as part of your work, unless you are

an accountant or a CFO, reflect on your financial literacy capabilities and always be honest with yourself on this issue.

3. While the duty of directors to exhibit care and diligence in discharging their duties is embedded firmly in the *Corporations Act*[12] and the common law, the Australian Securities and Investments Commission (ASIC) has also provided some clear guidelines regarding their expectation of our country's directors, including that which applies to financial literacy: these attributes include scepticism and accounting knowledge.

As mentioned earlier, this book is not here to teach you how to discharge your director's duties, including those relating to insolvency, approving or overseeing the financials, or in any other area relating to the company. That's a matter for your private and separate study. However, it's just such an important element when considering your board appointment that I couldn't overlook the opportunity to bring it to your attention. I talk more about directors' duties later in the book.

Some of the aforementioned topics can be researched via the internet on the company's website, in their annual report or submissions to regulators or public hearings, consultations, etc., or through your contacts prior to meeting with the chairman or CEO.

Sometimes specialist recruitment agencies are used by boards that are time-poor or wish to recruit a very narrowly-defined or difficult to secure skill-set. Or it may be that the board is seeking to recruit from a particular market that is not easily accessed by the company's staff or contacts. These agencies may also be used when the appointment is commercially- or politically-sensitive, so you may find yourself dealing with other parties first in the run up to meeting with the chairman or CEO.

Otherwise you may need to wait until you step through further

---

[12] www.austlii.edu.au/au/legis/cth/consol_act/ca2001172/s180.html; s180 Care and Diligence; accessed 22nd March 2015

parts of the nomination or appointment process to gain access to financial and other pertinent information. What is important is that regardless of when you actually get to see and review the information you need, you DO NOT sign your Consent to Act before you complete these checks. If reviewing the financials is not possible, your risk-radar should be immediately on alert, and further questions need to be asked.

It doesn't matter if the board has approved your appointment prior to you undertaking these checks and balances – until you sign that Consent to Act nothing is a done deal.

Warning: be careful of your own shadow

Be very careful should you be asked to attend all board or board committee meetings of a company that does not wish to appoint you officially to the board (via a Consent to Act), but which provides you with all meeting packs, access to other directors and the executives, AND (here's the kicker) deliberately seeks out and acts upon your advice regarding board decisions. There are special sets of definitions for arrangements of this type – what the law deems to be *de facto directors*.

These are persons who are legally accountable and obligated to the company for matters such as insolvency, just as is the case for properly appointed directors.[13,14] There are exceptions to these descriptions but you need to be on high alert if you find yourself in this position, either at the request of a chairman or if you have organically crossed over into this space through your relationship with the board.

Sometimes the people who ask you to undertake this type of role do not always understand the legal repercussions for you as an

---

[13] Section 9, Definition of Director, *Corporations Act 2001;* www.austlii.edu.au/au/legis/cth/consol_act/ca2001172/s9.html; accessed 28th September 2014

[14] www.findlaw.com.au/articles/1992/to-whom-do-directors-duties-apply.aspx; "To whom do Directors Duties Apply", Allan Topp and Tim James; accessed 28th September 2014

individual in this situation, or for the company. But sometimes they do and there could be a very good reason for you being put into this position, e.g. the board is restricted to undertaking further appointments but desparately needs your expertise or capabilities around their board table.

If you currently attend board meetings of a company, and your activities and contributions fit the above description, BUT you are neither a validly-appointed director nor a member of the company's executive, are you at risk? Is there an expectation (paid or otherwise) that you attend and opine on the decisions of that board or its committees (to which there is evidence that you are an influence)? If the answer is 'yes' and you are not a corporate law, professional adviser or governance expert, then take immediate legal advice on how you can remove yourself from this set up or be protected from it. There have been cases of people who have put themselves unwittingly into these very sticky situations, and who have paid the price accordingly, i.e. been held to account for the insolvency of a company or for other breaches of directors' duties notwithstanding they never signed a Consent to Act, nor had been officially appointed as a director by the board.

It's one of the greyest areas you can drift into around the board table, so be alert to this.

That's not to say that people and companies won't willingly and deliberately put themselves into this position if it suits their particular corporate set up. Protections can be built into your role here and your 'appointment', e.g. via the company's directors and officers (D&O) insurance policies, or via contractual provisions. Understand, however, that no matter what the company promises you in terms of protection, you can't contract out of the law under any circumstances and so in certain unsavoury times, those provisions won't save you from your actual legal liability if you are found to be a de facto director.

3

MEET THE PLAYERS

STILL IN THE pre-appointment stage, you are now ready to meet the game's key players. In fact, many of the answers to questions raised in the first two chapters will be discovered only when you have had a chance to talk to key board members and company executives; top of the ranks should be:

- The chairman
- The chief executive officer (CEO)
- The chief financial officer (CFO) (not everyone will meet this person, but I highly recommend it).

(See also Chapter 13, Key Relationships, for a broader consideration of these roles once you have been appointed.) It is also recommended that you seek out (where appropriate to do so) the experience and opinion of current and former board members. Other parties will come into play post-appointment.

It is at this point you should expect the company to ask you to enter into a confidentiality agreement regarding the conversations about to take place and/or documentation to be provided, as part of the due diligence. Be sure to read the agreement very carefully before signing it

– don't get over-excited and just sign it because it signals the company has an interest in you.

You must understand the company's expectations of you during the information exchange period, how long the agreement lasts, and any other important conditions. Be super sure to understand any restrictive covenants and those which could look to have a flow-on effect to your current employed role or other future opportunities in this sector. For example, are you being exposed to all sorts of very sensitive market and financial information about a company that could affect your current employment or ability to join other boards of the same industry? If in doubt take legal advice.

The chairman

I use the title "chairman" in my discussions about boards, purely because it is my natural way of describing the role. Others in the industry share this preference, but just as many are offended by it or prefer other terms, given the inference that it refers to a male only. Others prefer to use "chair" or "chairperson" (or "chairwoman" for females). When I use the word "chairman" I'm not denoting a person's gender in any way, and I consider it a gender-neutral description of the role.

At this point in your due diligence, you must meet with the chairman in the flesh (unless it is categorically impossible due to time zones, geographical limitations or some other impediment). With subsequent meetings you may be able to be more flexible and meet by telephone or perhaps by Skype. You should feel comfortable asking to meet with the chairman more than once if appropriate for the type of appointment and the type of board.

Don't EVER miss this step regardless of how you were nominated or how big/small the company is. The chairman is a critical window into matters such as:

- The board and its history
- The board's strengths, challenges and weaknesses
- The company's culture and values
- Quality of the board's operations and secretariat
- The underlying strategic, financial, regulatory and operational fundamentals of the company or group.

And, going back to points in earlier chapters, the chairman knows why the appointment has arisen.

Regardless of how the company goes about it, make it your business to insist on meeting the chairman (at least once in the flesh) prior to moving on to more critical due diligence stages.

Your meeting with the chairman is the ideal opportunity to ask all of those questions you have accumulated so far and which you are unable to move beyond without their insights and input. If the chairman believes that a more expeditious or fulsome response to any of your questions may be achieved by meeting with another director or a member of the executive, staff or volunteers, then they will let you know.

Meeting the chairman for the first time is a magic opportunity for you both to understand whether your appointment will be the right fit for the board and the company. You each need to be honest, though cordial, in how delicate subjects are addressed. This is one meeting that you want to be getting the good vibes from – your intuition needs to be in fully switched on here, to ensure you properly understand what is being said, and why. A great chairman will divulge appropriate details and information about the company and the board, to provide you with a clear understanding of what it is you might be about to enter into.

Go into this meeting with a list of predetermined questions on things that you believe are key to you moving to the next step, but also listen attentively to each cue they give you during the conversation.

If you do sense a significant amount of hesitation from the chairman on any one matter, or you feel as though they are holding back on any really important matters that are critical to your due diligence, then either:

- Call them on it at the meeting (politely and professionally)
- If it's uber-critical and a deal-breaker, let it pass in the conversation and consider raising it later in a follow-up discussion.

If a chairman is hiding or withholding information from the get-go, it could mean trouble lies ahead – though be careful when jumping to conclusions. Boards which are well placed to actively and openly engage when recruiting new directors will usually have a chairman with the ability to be as candid and forthcoming as you need them to be. If they aren't, then they have to be able to at least describe why they are coming up short on any particular topic.

You want to be able to have a great conversation with your future chairman as this is someone who will feature very strongly during your tenure with the company, and to whose direction the board's operations and effectiveness are subject. (I discuss your longer-term relationship, i.e. post-appointment with the chairman, in coming chapters, including how their role differs to that of the other directors.)

As I recommend for the CEO meeting to follow, you should test for yourself with regard to the chairman – who is this person? What is their history on this board? Can you see yourself working alongside them potentially for a very long time should you enjoy an ongoing tenure? What sort of vibe do they give you, person to person?

It's very important not to be overwhelmed about meeting the

chairman. (Remember my earlier comment that we all put our pants on the same way?) Yes, the chairman holds a pivotal role on the board and within the company and, depending on the board in question, the chairman could be a very high-profile or experienced company director or business person in their own right, but don't let that hold you back from asking the questions that you need to, to allow you to take your enquiries to the next level.

Depending on the constitution of the company and/or the charter of the board, this person *may* have the authority to have a casting vote in qualifying circumstances – so work towards determining whether he or she is someone you can be a fellow director with, purposefully and professionally.

A curve ball, but an important thought here – how dependent is the board on this particular chairman, in terms of its effective operations, ability to access funding (if it is a charity) or depth of board experience? If the chairman upped sticks and left what would it mean for the residual board?

Some chairmen can be seen as absolutely critical to the ongoing success and strength of the board. They may have the ability to attract and retain high-quality directors, or they may have external connections or access to resources which were you to lose them would be exceedingly difficult or highly disruptive to the board (and potentially the company). Others are very strong, experienced and highly-valued chairmen in their own right, but commercially they could be replaced with manageable disruption to the board (if the departure was sudden). It's just something to deliberate on as you move through this important phase of your due diligence. Some people will consider joining or leaving a board on the basis of who the chairman is. Others will not contemplate this.

Meeting the chairman is also a golden opportunity for you to be endorsed by them to the residual board and management, at least as far as the company taking the next step with you is concerned. It would be – in my opinion and experience – a hard task indeed (and a terribly surprising outcome) for a director to be appointed to a board if the chairman was not a fan of the person concerned (regardless of the appointment mechanisms of the company).

☑ MEETING THE CHAIRMAN CHECKLIST

☐ You must meet the chairman in person

☐ You should feel comfortable to ask for more than one meeting if necessary

☐ Explore their history with the company and as chairman

☐ Ask the chairman about why the board opening became available: depending on their answer, explore this further with due respect to the circumstances of your nomination and/or recent company history

☐ Look at how the chairman approached the discussion on culture, strategy and risk – did they unilaterally raise these topics, or was it up to you to do so?

☐ Look for openness, confidence, vision and transparency (this can be gleaned from the consideration given to their answers and whether their answers differ from anything else you've already learned or know about the company)

☐ Test their thoughts on the CEO and the executives (the CEO is the key)

☐ What does the chairman believe to be the company's greatest strengths, challenges, opportunities and threats?

☐ How do they view the financial viability of the organisation?

☐ How prominently does risk (and risk culture) figure in their discussion with you?

☐ As a person how do they strike you? Does he or she have outward strong leadership characteristics?

☐ Are there any impediments or other issues that would prevent you from accepting the appointment if you are eventually approved by the board – either on your side or theirs?

☐ Any there any conflicts of interest you feel you should declare or have brought to their attention? If so they should absolutely come out to the fore now.

Meeting the CEO

The chief executive officer (CEO) is appointed by the board, so during your directorship the board will need to make an assessment of this person's capabilities, performance contributions and whether they remain the right person to lead the company – both in the near- and long-terms. CEO succession planning by the board is a critical task but can be a forgotten exercise. Appointing the CEO is up there at the top of the list of things that boards are directly accountable for.

It would be highly preferable in my opinion to meet the CEO after you meet the chairman. Meet the CEO in private without any other party present. Only then can you have a very open and frank (but respectful and inquisitive) discussion with them regarding the company and indeed the board. It also allows you to ask questions that you may hesitate to raise in the company of others.

Meeting privately gives the CEO an opportunity to ask you a number of questions about what you understand about the company and where it's heading, or to just sound you out on your experience, your motives for joining the board and understanding what's drawn you to the opportunity.

If you happen to have a particular area of expertise that the board was actively seeking out – and you knew this going in – (for example, you may have clinical, financial, technology, digital or large-scale project experience, anything but obviously something in which the board is deficient or needs to strengthen), this meeting could be really important. In these circumstances, the CEO is likely to be working through your capabilities to appreciate your suitability for the role, given where the company is heading.

So make sure you have done your research and are ready with your questions. Confidently assume that the CEO will be one key cog in the company's due diligence of the nominees.

If you are trying to make an appointment to meet the CEO, and are continually being re-scheduled or assigned to meet someone else, that might signal an issue at play for you to be alert to. A CEO who doesn't prioritise the time to meet with potential incoming directors would be a concern from my point of view. Could it be reflective of their relationship with the board or the previous director (who you are replacing)? All CEOs are hideously busy and each circumstance is bespoke for its own reason but this is an important part of their role – regardless of the size of the company – and so you should expect a decent length meeting be afforded to you at this stage.

There may be companies that for some reason do not advocate that new or prospective directors meet the CEO pre-appointment (they prefer to keep appointments strictly arms-length and exclusive to the board). If that is the case explore why and determine whether you are comfortable with the answers given. Listen to the facts and your intuition; if necessary take guidance from a trusted mentor, preferably another experienced director. Does that seem right to you?

Meeting the CEO gives you the chance to ask the questions in the checklist below (as well those which arise out of the course of the discussion). Endeavour to seek out their thoughts on these matters.

☑ **MEETING THE CEO CHECKLIST**

☐ How does/can the CEO articulate the company's values?

☐ Explore the company's culture from the CEO's point of view – how is it attributed throughout the company? What or who influences the culture? Who has responsibility for it?

☐ How do they see the company's strategy for the next six to 12 months, three, five and ten years?

☐ What are the top five challenges and opportunities for the company (or the corporate group) – short and longer term?

☐ Have the CEO describe the company's risk management capabilities and risk culture – how's resourcing in this area? Is it constrained for any one reason? (It could be that their human risk capabilities are very strong and well-resourced or they could be significantly under-done: you just need to get a feel for where the company's investment in this capability is at, before making judgment or taking the questions further.)

☐ Can the CEO discuss the company's risk appetite and what is it influenced by. How often is it reviewed by the board?

☐ Have the CEO describe the experience and calibre of the executives and senior management.

☐ How does the CEO view the financial position of the company or group? What do they see as the company's challenges regarding retaining or attaining long-term financial sustainability?

☐ How would the CEO describe the company's recognition of, investment in and commitment to, corporate governance?

☐ Where is the company at with IT, social media and digital (strategies and capabilities)?

☐ Are there any major litigations, government or regulatory reviews underway, anticipated or with the potential to arise in the coming 12 months? If yes, are these standard and recurring reviews (related to normal prudential programs or licence reviews), or is the review or litigation arising linked to a particular past event?

☐ How well does management interact with the board? How would the CEO describe the quality and robustness of this relationship?

☐ What is the company's approach or commitment to CSR (corporate social responsibility) and ESG (environment, social, governance)?

☐ As a CEO, what keeps them awake at night?

This is not an exhaustive list by any means as you can imagine just how important context is here – it's everything really. Think company size, type of industry, etc.

Getting through these topics as part of your conversation with the CEO will either whet your appetite to continue on your due diligence journey (as what you've heard is either hugely encouraging or totally understandable given the right context), or you are cumulatively coming to the conclusion that perhaps you need to re-think or reflect on this opportunity. No-one can make this decision for you. You have to rely on your commercial and governance experience, intuition and the impressions that you've formed to this point.

Recalling the discussion in the chairman's section, from a human perspective, ask yourself who is this person (the CEO) and what motivates him or her? How dependent is the company and the shareholders on retaining this particular CEO to deliver on agreed short- and long-term performance goals?

This is obviously not a question for the CEO but it is an element to keep in mind because both large corporates and very small companies indeed can be impacted tremendously if the CEO is a key person risk, and without them the company might well be cactus or fall into a whole world of pain very quickly. There's nothing you can do about it per se as an individual director, especially coming into the game, but be alert to this point in your own mind as you work your way through your residual due diligence and beyond into the boardroom.

> **CAUTION:** *While your conversation with both the CEO and chairman will inevitably lead you to other lines of questioning about the company, you would be advised not to conclude either meeting without clearly understanding the board and company's attitudes towards workplace health and safety. Given the potential director liability attached to this topic, if it comes up short of your expectations in your discussions, be sure to make further enquiries about it because key deficiencies in this area could spell high stakes for your future directorship of this company.*

Further questions and relevant issues for the CEO and chairman will continue to be flagged in the coming sections, so keep this in mind cumulatively as we move beyond these two parties and onto other recommended steps in the process.

Meeting the CFO

Where the board's process allows, it's my personal belief that you should also meet the chief financial officer (CFO) or their equivalent. This is the person who controls the cash, assets, access to and use of the company's credit and is responsible for reporting the status of such things to you in the financials periodically (the sign-off of which cannot be abdicated to any persons other than the directors). That's a pretty important person in the scheme of things, particularly given the risks and liabilities involved with insolvency and your director's duties generally.

Even the smallest of companies has someone who manages the accounts, loans, assets, cash flows, investments, etc., so why shouldn't this person be on your radar? Take a copy of the financials with you when you meet the CFO (or equivalent) and make sure you have been right through them prior to this meeting. If you haven't yet been provided with these documents, ensure that the CFO brings them to the meeting so you can step through any elements you are unsure of or want to become more familiar with at a later point.

Test with them any parts you don't understand. Given that this could be a brand new industry to you, it's critical that you are comfortable with how the accounts are structured, that you understand how the cash flows work and how the debt is structured.

Ask the CFO or their equivalent to step you through any key issues to note in your shoes as a director potentially coming into this company.

Don't ever feel intimidated by the CFO or the idea of their role – especially if you've had little to no experience with financials and the company you might be joining is of a significant size. You are allowed to be confident of your own merits going into this discussion, and it's not to say the CFO will be expecting first-class accounting or financial brilliance from you. Expectations should be relative to their knowledge of you, your background, the type of company and the complexity of the accounts. However, if the accounts are intricate, complex or just plain overwhelming, you need to be upfront with the CFO and openly discuss how far your capabilities extend.

This is an important meeting because:

1. You get to sound out and delve into topics that will inevitably help you to understand the business more acutely from the get-go.

2. If this is your first board appointment and you've yet to have any experience with financials, it will also provide you with requisite insight into whether you are ready to take on this or any other director appointment (at this time, 'sans' further training).

The discussion and your review of the company's financials should make you feel either more or less sure of its solvency.

Meeting the CFO is a gift of an opportunity for you. This person has to give the board assurance regarding the robustness of the company's accounting and financial systems, and the capabilities of the people who oversee them. If relevant to the appointment and the company concerned, you might also enquire about the audit process, audit plan (if any) and who the current auditors are (particularly if you are being touted for a future audit committee posting).

✔ CFO CHECKLIST

- ☐ Can you read and understand the financials? If not, is it because of their complexity and volume, or is it because your financial literacy doesn't allow you to?
- ☐ Financial ratios – how do these appear? Are there any overt trends for you to be aware of?
- ☐ Understand what are the relevant ratios for this industry and business
- ☐ Check and read the Notes to the Accounts and question anything not understood
- ☐ Request information on how and when the company pays PAYG and other taxes
- ☐ Check on superannuation for employees – are payments up to date? Who has responsibility for making these payments?
- ☐ Are there any outstanding taxes?

☐   Are there any signs of cashflow or balance sheet insolvency?

☐   Are you comfortable with how the accounts are structured? Do you understand the cashflows and how the debt is structured/repaid?

☐   As CFO, what keeps you awake at night?

Meeting other directors

Meeting at least one or two current (or just resigned/retired) directors is also recommended pre-appointment as part of your due diligence. This step can be seen by some directors and CEOs as wonderfully proactive and a reflection of your commitment to this appointment opportunity; others might see it as over the top, or inappropriate if the appointment is to a very small company or a particularly public or well-known company. Ignore the nay-sayers – if the appointment process allows for it, why wouldn't you do this? I would, every time.

The board should be very open and welcoming to incoming or nominated directors who wish to meet up with one or two of those who are already in (or have just exited from) the fold. It will provide you with yet another great opportunity to gather information about the board's operations, history and collegiality. Meeting with these directors can provide you with an insight into cultural attributes of the company and the board, and other matters that may have come up in your meetings with the CEO and chairman.

Test the directors on how they see the company's commitment towards occupational health and safety and corporate governance against that shared with you by the chairman and CEO. Are there issues with the financials, past or future financial performance, other major risks/issues/insights? If they were in your shoes, what would be the key things they would discuss/raise/reflect on?

If currently appointed, are these directors people you can see yourself spending many hours with, and with whom you'll be happy or prepared to stand side by side with in the trenches of this boardroom? Exercise both your personal and commercial nous here – read the situation and gauge how best to ask your questions to your satisfaction.

> **CAUTION:** *Your 'fit' with the board is important – no matter how great either you or they look on paper, if together you are not 'simpatico' you may be in for some long and arduous days ahead.*

Don't underestimate board and cultural 'fit' as part of your due diligence. The board will certainly be considering 'fit' (or it should be) as part of their review of final nominations and appointment recommendations. It doesn't mean you all have to be best mates – but you need to be comfortable that there's a reasonable level of professional courtesy and respect among the director group, and that everyone understands why it is that they are sitting around that particular boardroom table together.

4

ROUNDING OFF YOUR
DUE DILIGENCE

LET'S JUST RECAP on your progress so far in the pre-appointment due diligence process. Each of the conversations we've discussed up to this point should have:

- Allowed you to see whether the company has actually taken the time and committed the resources needed to properly consider, identify, review and respond to its challenges and opportunities.

- Informed you how sophisticated (or otherwise) the company is in determining its strategy and the execution of same, as well as how resourced, financial and planned the company is in regard to these elements. This will provide an insight into where the pressure points are (or could come from) and to see if the company spends demonstrably more time on these issues relative to others.

- Allowed you to reflect on how agile and flexible the company might be in meeting future challenges and opportunities (be they internally or externally driven).

- Confirmed whether the company is truly forward-looking, or lives in the past off borrowed strategies.

You would also hope your due diligence tells you how researched and ready the company is regarding possible future disruptions in the industry, where these might come from and when. Hopefully, it also outlines what the company's response to such disruptions would be if they eventuated, or what steps the company is taking now to stop, impede, counter or slow their impact. In taking this road, I might draw the ire of some who might think that the following areas are extending one's due diligence beyond what's necessary and appropriate. However, for me they most certainly come into their own on a very strong basis.

Technology, risk management and risk culture, senior management capabilities and experience – I can see how some people might think of these as three topics too many to ask after. But do yourself a favour and enquire about them anyway – contemplate them in the context of the company you are being considered for. Information gained about these elements will always be the cherry on top of your very delicious due diligence cake. Personally I'm a big fan of the cherry…

Technology

A super important concept to be discussing with the company (definitely with the chairman and CEO) is technology. Get a good feel for what's contemplated with technology. Without a doubt, for every business going around, technology is (and will continue to be) both a massive opportunity and challenge on various fronts. People's capabilities, understanding of and experience with technology is madly varied and this in itself can present interesting challenges and dilemmas for companies and boards deciding where to invest their IT capital.

I'm no IT expert – ask anyone who's worked with me for five minutes and they'll attest to this. My point is that 'technology' and 'IT' can mean many, many things to different people. In fact, I've recently heard that the concept of 'IT' is so 1990s, and that the world has markedly moved on to newer descriptions. Regardless of what's the right (read 'cool') terminology to use, just start with the word 'IT' and go from there. If it's to be described otherwise, someone will soon let you know! This is handy to know going on to boards or doing your pre-appointment due diligence, as you want to be sure that you are all talking about the same thing when the topic comes up.

As part of your due diligence steps, ensure that the concept of technology either rates as a priority or is a recognised component of the company's strategy, risks or recognised future opportunities.

☑ IT CHECKLIST

Key questions and considerations might include:

- ☐ What is happening technology-wise in the company?
- ☐ What are its current IT capabilities (human and otherwise)?
- ☐ Are there major works programs underway or planned to ensure the company remains technologically advanced or can improve in the future?
- ☐ How far down the list is technology (and this includes digital capabilities) as a strategic priority (and depending on the company size would it warrant even being on this list)?
- ☐ Is there a technology and innovation department, and/or a board committee which oversees IT development and major projects? In the management ranks, is there a chief technology officer or equivalent?
- ☐ Are any of the directors technology experts or highly skilled in this area?
- ☐ Do the company's IT projects typically run on time and on budget? What's been the track record here?

Remember, context, context, context will be important. But these are great questions to ask nonetheless.

Risk management capabilities and risk culture

There used to be a saying at one of my old workplaces that I'm a big fan of and that was that **risk was everyone's business**. I've never heard a better description of it since. It describes just how important it is that every single person in an organisation understands what risk means, how it impacts or forms part of their role, and what responsibility they have in identifying, managing or mitigating it. From the receptionist to the chairman, risk quite simply must be everyone's business. Risk culture is the seamless embedding of risk consideration and contemplation into a company's every-day working life.

In undertaking your due diligence, you MUST check where this company is at with their commitment to risk management and risk culture.

You can have the most flash, grand, well-researched, insightful bells-and-whistles strategy or business plan set down for the company (and approved by the board) but without a strong, identifiable and embedded (risk) culture, the company is exposed and so is the board (that's code for YOU). A known or systemic point of weakness in the company is usually going to bite it every time – and risk is no different. Just as the tone from the top is a major influence on the company's culture generally, so it is also for risk.

✔ **RISK CHECKLIST**

☐ You want to understand what the company does to embed risk culture into the organisation, how it is defined, how the risk appetite is set, how often it's reviewed and what the capabilities are within the risk function.

- [ ] Due to the size and circumstances of the company, is risk a tack-on to someone else's role (wherein the incumbent is really not that well-credentialed to be running with this speciality)? Or conversely, is the risk function highly resourced, and managed by someone who is deeply experienced and super credentialed?

- [ ] Look at the size and complexity of the company, does the risk capability, infrastructure and investment (in people, training and systems) fit with what you'd expect in an organisation of its type?

- [ ] When were the risk systems and capabilities last audited or formally reviewed by the board?

- [ ] How does the board set risk appetite and how often is it reviewed? Does it even embrace the concept of risk appetite?

What you're trying to do with this line of questioning is to get underneath the skin or fabric of the company's risk culture and capabilities. You really want to have an understanding of what the current lay of the land is in this space, as this is by far one of the most important features of your due diligence.

Risk is definitely to be considered in the context of the organisation. If you are joining your first board and coming from an executive background of highly sophisticated and developed systems, risk culture and capability, then going onto the board of a very small operating entity or a company which is still maturing its risk standards and learnings, will likely require you to adjust your professional expectations of what you may find. On the flip-side, small companies can sometimes bring the loveliest of surprises with regard to their level of risk engagement, while disappointingly, large companies can sometimes be under-done in this area.

Notwithstanding where the company is on the risk spectrum, you still need to get a sense of how risk is understood, identified and managed. You never know what you'll find – size and balance sheet will not be a give-away on how the company approaches risk.

A dialogue here with your chairman and CEO will be insightful, as will be a discussion with the company secretary who can usually give a very balanced view of risk management in the company.

What you are hoping to hear from your discussions with these parties is that:

- Risk culture and risk systems are recognised and valued assets of the company.

- Risk should be considered an enabler of the organisation (not something to be feared, or which restricts or encumbers taking well-considered business decisions).

- Risk is managed to a professional standard relative to the company's size and complexity, their resources and what they understand to be best practice.

- Risk is an inherent and conscious consideration when planning major changes to the company's strategy, market positioning or business plan. If it's not, or is not expressly recognised in this way, is that something you can bring to the table as a value-add to the board?

- There is evidence that if risk is well recognised and understood in the company it is dynamic (i.e. it's not static and a tick-the-box operational element).

Invest in these discussions about risk, they are important components in your due diligence efforts and in getting to know the company.

Quality, experience and calibre of the executives and senior management

Giving consideration to the experience, credentials and diversity of the executive/senior management team is definitely important when reviewing the landscape of a company. These are the people who are at the coalface operating the company; they are the ones implementing and (hopefully) delivering the strategy approved by the board; they are the ones in charge of the money, investments, the company's reputation, legal position, and the assets and liabilities on a daily basis. They will be doing the physical steering of the ship – far, far away from the latitude and longitude of your seat in the boardroom.

You wouldn't (and shouldn't) want to go into a board appointment blind on details about the senior management.

Start with the internet. Check the company's website for a description of the executive team. Get a feel for their experience, qualifications, achievements, specialisations, where they fit into the company, etc. If there's no information on the site regarding management, you should ask yourself why. Even very small companies often have this information listed, but it may be that the company's operations don't warrant this, so enquire if it's missing if there is a good reason why.

When meeting with the CEO (either for the first or second time but definitely prior to appointment), ensure that you include in your discussion, questions for them about the experience and capabilities of the executive:

• What is tenure like – is there a high turnover?
• What are the capability gaps that exist with the current group?
• What are their greatest strengths?
• What's the relationship like between the executive and the CEO?

- Is there any history to be aware of so you don't miss a particular nuance during a future board conversation?
- Is there sufficient succession planning for key or very senior roles, such that the risk of losing a key person can be managed if it ever eventuated without notice?
- How are the executives remunerated?
- Are there any key-person risks that the organisation is aware of in terms of the executive set?

This is not an exhaustive list but it is a good place to get the conversation started from. Some of these topics may come up in your discussions with the chairman organically, or you might reserve a couple for them specifically to get their view.

The level and extent of detail you go into is entirely dependent on the size of the company and all of its variables (complexity, location, industry competitiveness, talent pools, remuneration levels). So plan your questions accordingly but, remember, the executive and senior management teams are absolutely critical to the delivery of the strategy and the business plan of the company. They are also responsible for successfully embedding a strong culture throughout the organisation, delivering sustainable financial returns and ensuring that the company has dynamic and well-managed risk systems.

While the board ultimately approves and monitors the company's strategy, robustness of risk systems, financial integrity and culture of the organisation, from an everyday point of view it's the executives, CEO and senior management team who deliver the goods on the ground. Getting that part of the equation right is absolutely critical to the company reaching its potential to remain a long-term, sustainable enterprise.

5

JUST A LITTLE BIT MORE...
BUT IT'S WORTH IT

GOSH, THE ROAD to directorship is a long one, isn't it? And you're not even on the board yet! How much more arduous can and should this be?

For your context (although I hope not comfort) there would definitely be people who join boards each year who will undertake extremely few, if any of the steps outlined to you so far. This might be due to a whole host of reasons, perhaps due to their genuine confidence about:

- The financial and historical strength of the company (what could possibly go wrong?)
- Getting the chance to join a nationally or regionally iconic company's board overrides any sense to undertake proper due diligence (they're happy to take their chances)
- The fact that the company or corporate group has millions (even perhaps billions) of dollars sitting behind it and that with all that cash and assets, nothing seriously could go wrong (or if it did, there's tonnes of money in the pot to support a failure)

- Conversely, if the company is tiny and it tips over, no-one will notice and it won't be a blight on anyone's record
- Given the company concerned, undertaking proper due diligence would seem trivial, or it may indicate to the rest of the board that you could be a problematic, overly-nervous future director
- You've been nominated by your employer or other connection group to be appointed to this company's board and to undertake such an extensive due diligence would indicate an ungratefulness for the opportunity, or somehow reflect your lack of confidence in the organisation.

Well, these reasons might well be fine for *those* directors, but you wouldn't have made it this far in the book if you weren't the diligent and considered type who actually took the prospect of being a company director seriously.

The reality of it is that apparent corporate strength, or being considered an iconic company in its relevant neck of the woods, won't save your skin in the courts, with the press or with the country's regulators, if you or your board gets into a situation because no-one did their homework or everyone's eyes were snapped shut.

So hang tight, these are the last of the due diligence steps.

Items to consider on your way to reaching for your pen to sign the Consent to Act are:

- The corporate structure
- The constitution, board and committee charters
- Directors insurance
- Deeds of access, insurance and indemnity
- Board calendars that are left to run.

Corporate structure

It's really important that you understand the basic corporate structure of the business, i.e.:

- Is it the only company in the corporate structure, or is the company a parent entity to other companies?
- If it's a parent company how many subsidiaries does it have (and where are they located?).
- Is the entity owned by a parent company (therefore it's a subsidiary) and if so, is the parent domestic or based overseas? What does that mean for your board's role, it's legal and governance responsibilities?
- What is the legal construct of the company? Is it a public or proprietary company, a small or large proprietary company? Is it limited by shares or guarantees? Is it an unlimited guarantee company?
- Does your company contract with the parent or subsidiary in any way? How different are the corporate cultures? And what are the synergies between the entities? What binds them together as a group or conglomerate? Are the strategies and business plans interwoven, co-dependent or wholly independent?

In terms of corporate structure, you can make a lot of these checks by doing a company search on the ASIC website. This will also tell you (for a very small fee) who the current directors and shareholders are, where and when the company was incorporated, how often and when the shareholders or directors have changed and what the shareholding percentages are.

I like doing a company search very early on in the due diligence process (I do this also for companies I am interviewing to work for) because for not much dosh, it gives you a lot of pertinent facts about the entity and will feed into your discussions with the chairman, CEO and CFO – particularly if the corporate structure is complex or there have been a lot of director and shareholding changes in just a short period.

The company secretary or chief legal counsel (if they have one) will also be able to confirm these details for you.

Company constitution

Definitely get a copy of the company's constitution. Sometimes, depending on the company, this document can be found on the internet, but if not the company secretary will be able to email it to you. A company will have a constitution or a set of replaceable rules[15] or a combination of both. Whatever its form, you want a copy!

Some people may think I'm being pedantic here by requesting a copy of and reading the constitution but consider this: outside of the law of the land, this is the company's ultimate rule book (giving a run for its money to the board charter which is one of the board's other rule books). My point is that this document is incredibly powerful and important, relative to the company's existence, and actions cannot be taken by the board in breach of the constitution. What's more, when you join this board you are entering into a contract.

The constitution is a contract that binds the company and each of its members, the company and each director and secretary, and member to member[16]. It sets out how the company is governed.

Imagine the importance of this document to your shareholders and stakeholders. It is a document that new directors should definitely make it their business to read at least once. The following are just some of the types of topics that it might cover[17]:

- Directors' meetings, appointments, removal, contracts, remuneration
- The passing of resolutions
- Annual general meetings (AGMs) and general shareholder meetings
- Extraordinary meetings, meeting notices, indemnities
- Voting at members and board meetings

---

[15] www.austlii.edu.au/cgi-bin/sinodisp/au/legis/cth/consol_act/ca2001172/s135.html?stem=0&synonyms=0&query=replaceable%20rules; accessed 2nd October 2014
[16] www.austlii.edu.au/au/legis/cth/consol_act/ca2001172/s140.html; accessed 28th March 2015
[17] www.companyp.com.au/prod/pdf/shelf_sample_constitution.pdf; accessed 2nd October 2014

- How the accounts are to be kept, capital raisings, share transfers
- Amendments to the constitution
- Auditor appointments, borrowing powers, use of the company seal
- Related-party transactions, trustee relationships, winding up proceedings
- Any restriction clauses.

As you can see, the constitution carries significant clout relative to most other documents in the company's possession. In fact, it's probably the granddaddy of them all, bar the initial application for incorporation (there's no party without that one). So you can see why I'm extremely encouraging of you to get a copy.

If the company is a subsidiary, also ask whether it is contracted by its constitution to act in the best interests of its parent. Check out s187 of the *Corporations Act*[18] to understand this in its entirety as there are qualifying criteria for this to hold. If yes, what does this mean for how the company is operated and governed (a great question for your CEO or company secretary)? This can be common in corporate groups with numerous special-purpose entities which are also majority-owned.

Board charters and governance policies

When you think the time is right (some will think pre-appointment, others will say 'post'), ask for a copy of the company's key governance policies, as well as all board and committee charters unless these are published on the internet.

The board charter in particular is incredibly important as it sets out the road rules for how the board operates on a day-to-day basis. This document generally sets out the role of the board, its authority (and where that's derived from), its responsibilities and any restrictions, how

---

[18] www.austlii.edu.au/cgi-bin/sinodisp/au/legis/cth/consol_act/ca2001172/s187.html?stem=0&synonyms=0&query=subsidiary

and when it meets, quorums and voting structures, the number of directors, who chairs the board and how often the charter is reviewed.

It might also include what tasks the board can delegate to others and what powers it reserves. Your board's activities will be guided by the contents of the charter so definitely put this on your document acquisition list.

The company secretary will be the custodian of the board charter so any questions regarding its contents or application can be directed straight to them.

Are you allowed to see the minutes?

If you've signed a confidentiality agreement as part of your pre-appointment due diligence process, you will be able to gain access to a copy of the board's minutes (say from the last meeting back to three years). If the board's minutes are available for your review, absolutely get a copy. I cover later in detail how critical minutes are to the board and to you as an individual director. But if they are on offer at this point, grab them with both hands (just be absolutely sure you can safeguard them when they are in your possession as they are highly confidential documents).

Minutes will also reveal past or pending litigation or regulatory reviews, what's been keeping the board occupied over the past few years, and they will also show you what the board spends most of its time on. This could be significant strategy and financial matters, or compliance or frivolous issues, or any number of things. Is there a balance between what's considered strategically and operationally? What's the story being told?

Directors' insurance

You need more than just a love for the company and a good set of financials to make this gig work for you. You need to understand how you would be indemnified (if at all) by the company should something go wrong.

This could be by way of indemnification from the assets or it may take the form of insurance. Costs can accumulate (actually they skyrocket) at the drop of a poorly-reasoned hat. Legal bills can very quickly escalate with costs also accruing to reputation and for rectification or operational expenses and losses. And that's BEFORE you've even set foot inside the courtroom!

Asking about indemnity does not make you look like a spoiled, snooty director who wants their backside covered in the event of a disaster or breach; nor does (or should) it make you look nervous and unsure about the appointment. Director indemnification is a complex area of the law so needless to say I'm not going there in this book. However, this is a really important item for you to understand as a director, given that you could be personally sued while holding this directorship.

Indemnification can vary as widely as you could ever believe. Yes, you may be indemnified out of the company's or fund's assets (which is helpful if there are millions of dollars' worth of them to help out). Or you could be covered (in part or in full) by insurance policies that the company takes out on your behalf. When the chips are down and there's a matter afoot, you will want to know what your indemnification prospects are.

You should also want to know if there are things you can never be indemnified or insured for, e.g. fraud and wilful misconduct before you sign the bottom line. The *Corporations Act* prohibits a company from paying insurance premiums to cover wilful breaches and breaches of certain directors' duties involving an improper use of position or information obtained through a director's position in the company.

> **TIP:** *Ensure that as part of your due diligence you enquire about how the company insures its directors.*

You might reserve this line of questioning for the company secretary or chief counsel. Use your judgment from what you've learned so far and who you've met. Also, factor in the context of the company to determine when is the right time to raise this topic.

If the company does not have sufficient assets out of which it could indemnify you for actions and legal costs, or it doesn't have the money to pay for a directors and officers (D&O) insurance policy, it doesn't mean you have to bail on the opportunity. At a very basic level, D&O insurance provides cover for liabilities (and their associated defence costs) which may arise as part of law suits, class actions, regulatory and government reviews, or other investigations. Some companies may not be able to offer you any directors' liability insurance whatsoever. Other companies may simply wish to prioritise their cash for other purposes or will expect directors to fund their own cover. Others will have extremely comprehensive and professional cover which, bar you being a completely fraudulent or criminal director, or one who wilfully neglects their duties, will generally provide you with some insurance coverage in the time of crisis.

> **TIP:** *It is really important to understand your insurance cover. Some policies do not pay your legal bills until after the case is decided; others will provide coverage upfront. This is therefore an issue that reinforces the need to check this policy carefully or get advice on before signing the Consent to Act.*

At the time of writing this book, there was individual insurance cover available for purchase in Australia via brokers for directors who have to pay for their own insurance when their company won't or can't (or the policies that they do have are less than ideal). It's a great option to help you sleep at night as you get to choose the level of cover and premium paid. It's also personally tax deductible and you can cover any gaps found in the company's D&O policy.

You may not get access to the actual policy that the company has in place before you join. However, you need to ask some questions about the policy pre-appointment and understand its key terms and the scope of coverage before proceeding to consent.

> **WARNING:** *Remember, even the biggest or most robust insurance policy will not save you from the consequences that will arise from being found to be a wilfully deceitful or fraudulent director.*

Once you get hold of the policy and, if you can stomach it, give it a thorough read. Or ask your company secretary or the company's insurance broker to give you a layman's summary of the key elements. Some policies can be a simple bolt-on from other property or 'loss of income' type policies held by the company (so they were thrown in by the broker or insurer for just a little more premium), and they may not be worth the paper they are written on. Sometimes the person in the company charged with obtaining the policy (and even the other directors) doesn't really understand anything about them, nor what to look for when shopping for one.

While not an exhaustive list, things to look for in these D&O and other insurance policies of the company are:

- Whether the company can choose its own lawyers in a litigation
- Whether the company has to get permission to engage any lawyers

- Whether the limits noted for directors get lumped in with that for the company (if there is no separate defence costs cover for the board, a company's claims may well consume all the insured limits first before it gets to consider the directors' legal fees, etc.)

- Whether there are restrictions, covenants or exclusions that make the policy potentially untenable (maybe that's why it's cheap?)

- Check how and when defence costs are advanced for directors by the insurer (insurance won't do you much good if you have to sell your house to pay your legal bills only to be reimbursed at the end of the case).

Get some advice from your own or the company's insurance broker once you receive a copy of the policy (be it before or after appointment).

Assess your risk appetite relative to what's on offer from the policy, what you know about the company and the law, and then determine if there's a gap that should be closed through obtaining your own private cover. In the absence of what you believe is a credible and adequate policy, you should consider obtaining your own private insurance (which neither the company nor the other directors can access if you ever need to call upon it – it is all yours).

To wrap up this section, I've compiled a checklist for your consideration.

☑ D&O INSURANCE CHECKLIST

☐ Have a conversation with the company to understand their indemnity provisions (including any restrictions)

☐ Obtain a copy of the D&O policy to read thoroughly

☐ Will the company pay for external independent legal advice so you can properly understand the policy?

☐ Find out what's not included in the D&O policy

☐   Is there separate side cover exclusive for directors?

☐   Will the policy pay directors' legal costs upfront or only at the conclusion of the matter?

☐   When exactly does the policy 'kick in'?

☐   Does it feel as if you should be investigating taking out your own private cover?

Deeds of access, insurance and indemnity

A great number of companies with mature corporate governance systems and frameworks offer deeds of access, insurance and indemnity to their directors. The offer is made at the discretion of the company, but if offered to one director it will be offered to you all.

These deeds (legal documents) are bespoke to each company and are generally drawn up by the company's lawyers or in-house counsel. They can provide a number of advantages and benefits to directors beyond that afforded by the *Corporations Act* and the common law. They typically cover matters such as:

- Providing you with a greater than normal accessibility period or access rights to the company's books and records than that afforded by the *Corporations Act*

- The deed may compel the company to maintain directors' and officers' insurance cover for the board in perpetuity

- The deed may restrict the company's ability to amend their constitution for the period of the cover applicable to directors – particularly where that amendment would reduce the company's indemnification or rights of the directors

- They set out other relevant provisions regarding indemnification of directors from the company's assets.

There are usually also significant restrictions on amending the deed, i.e. if it changes for one director, it changes for all.

Again, really tiny, formative or resource poor companies may not offer these deeds. However, if a deed of this nature is offered to you, read it and, if you are comfortable with the contents, sign it and take up the offer. As a director, if such an offer were made to me (and it was a quality offering) I'd grab it with both hands.

Companies offering these deeds will usually also have the means to pay for any independent legal advice for directors regarding its contents, so if this opportunity is offered to you, seriously consider acccepting it and have the deed reviewed. Note that the deed may seek something from you in return, for example there may be special confidentiality provisions required to be adhered to.

The board's residual meeting schedule

It might sound a bit naff, but if you are contemplating joining a board and discover that you actually can't attend a substantial number of the remaining meetings in the board's calendar for the year, this can be a significant issue concerning your appointment. You will have to raise this very early on with your nominating party or the chairman. This is so that deliberations can be made between the parties on how this is going to impact the board until the next meeting calendar is determined. I'll spend more time on board calendars in the next chapters but for your first year's appointment, check this out ahead of time to ensure that you can actually physically get to these meetings (keeping this particularly in mind for boards which travel for meetings, or meet interstate from your home base).

Your constant inability to attend board meetings will very quickly tick off your fellow directors, company secretary and executive team. People expect you to check this detail going into appointments so don't miss this off your to-do list. If there are major clashes for the period left to run on the current board calendar, have a very early dialogue with your appointees about this – sometimes it can be explained to the board, executives and the secretariat that you may miss one meeting or you have to join it by telephone – just until the next board calendar comes around when your diary can be included in the mix when the next round of dates are being negotiated.

If it turns out that you cannot make a vast number of meetings until the calendar is refreshed, then the timing of this appointment may need re-assessment. It's neither fair nor acceptable to the company or its stakeholders for you to miss numerous board meetings during the first year of your tenure. You may also be in breach of your duty of care and diligence. And taking meetings by telephone is an entirely sub-optimal solution. Being on the end of a telephone and trying to interact and contribute to a board meeting (sometimes for hours) is arduous and often ineffective. And that's just at your end!

If you do need to join your new board for a couple of meetings from a distance, a video conference would be a much better solution. I touch on joining meetings by means other than in person later in the book.

You might be thinking right now that to get across everything I've covered to this point will be exhausting, or that it's over the top. It must seem like this due diligence stuff will take forever (do people really do all of this, I hear you say?).

Can I say in real life that you'll find the conversations on all of these points will run fairly organically and when you get started it will be like any other business conversation you would have with peers or colleagues. It seems as if the questions go on and on, and that it could be embarrassing for you to cover all these things with people you don't know and want to impress simultaneously. But don't be overwhelmed or put off by the effort required to have these conversations. As stated earlier, you'll never regret the research and quality inputs will lead to quality outputs. It is one thing to choose to skip some of the due diligence steps because of your own self-imposed reasons, it's another entirely not to do them at all because you had no idea in the first place that those items form part of a normal due diligence process.

Pre-appointment wrap up

We're now through what are generally recognised as the bigger ticket, pre-appointment matters. If you go into your appointment having covered off the items so far, then you will be in great shape and will have your eyes wide open as to what it is you've signed up for.

You wouldn't sign on the dotted line to join a company as an executive or specialist or CEO before doing thorough due diligence on the company, so why wouldn't you do the same when becoming a director? While you may not get a perfect run at all of the items and questions covered to this point, the important thing has been to bring them to your attention so that you can go in prepared and more comfortable than if you left it all to the gods!

You can wing it and leave it to chance and go in blind. And you know, maybe everything goes well and you come up trumps anyway. Lucky is what you'd be. I'd rather you made your own luck.

Appointment documentation

Before we leave this chapter and get onto other matters which assume your appointment has been crystallised, there are just a couple of issues I want to bring to your attention regarding appointment documentation.

It really does draw the ire and frustration (not to mention early disappointment) of the secretariat when you don't return the appointment documentation on time or complete it as requested. These are important documents for the company (for a whole host of reasons) and so if you are sent an information pack to read, complete and return by a designated due date, then please do the company a big favour and actually do this.

Sounds incredibly whingey I know, but it makes a great first impression on the secretariat (a big bonus which I'll discuss later) and it helps them to finalise the requisite checks and searches often needed to be done by a certain date, to make your appointment valid, or to allow the board to finalise its approval of your appointment.

Fit and proper checks with statutory and other authorities (if used) can take some time. If your appointment is subject to those checks coming back completed and satisfactory, and you haven't returned your forms in time, you may have to wait until the next board meeting comes around to be approved. It can be problematic for the board if you are filling a vacancy and they need your appointment to go through as scheduled.

It also sets the first impression internally about how committed and interested you really are in the appointment (be this a fair impression/assumption or otherwise); being slack and not returning your forms on time (or to the degree of completion required) sets a low starting mark for you in the secretariat and sometimes the CEO's office.

Also, if the secretariat needs your profile to put onto the company's internet site and they ask you to review and confirm the details proposed to be published, please do this as requested. If you are under some time restraints given other things going on in your life, let the secretariat know and they'll work with you to make it happen.

Make sure you give an accurate account of your address, telephone number and email; and of course return your signed Consent to Act. If there are any other points that you should confirm to the secretariat to ensure you are always contactable, then please do so, e.g. you have multiple residences, special contact numbers or procedures, or you can only have documents delivered in one particular place.

And finally, without question always ensure you tell the secretariat when you move house, as the company only has a certain number of days to tell ASIC (and sometimes other regulators) otherwise the company incurs a fine.

☑ **THE TOP 10 PRE-APPOINTMENT MUST-DOS**

*referring to detailed points provided in preceding chapters

☐ Internet research: the barbeque test; board composition, ASIC search, press coverage

☐ Reflections: how did this opportunity find you and why does the company need a new director?

☐ Read the financials: solvency test

☐ Are you sufficiently financially-literate to join this board?

☐ Draft your list of need-to-know questions on key areas:
  • Culture
  • OH&S
  • Strategy (opportunities, risks and threats)
  • Financials
  • The executive
  • Risk culture and capabilities
  • Technology.

☐ Meet the chairman

☐ Meet the CEO

☐ Meet the CFO

☐ Meet other directors (serving or just retired)

☐ Check:
  • Board calendar for residual year
  • Your indemnification – D&O insurance cover
  • The constitution and board charters
  • Governance policies, the minutes (if available).

A full pre-appointment checklist is given at the back of the book.

PART TWO

INVITATION ACCEPTED

In this part it's assumed that you have been approved to join the board (and you've graciously accepted the offer).

6

BOARDROOM INDUCTION

"Success is a science; if you have the conditions,
you get the result."

OSCAR WILDE[19]

CONGRATULATIONS! YOU'VE RECEIVED your invitation to join the board. You've completed your due diligence and are delighted to move forward with the opportunity. So, what next? I'm really hoping for your sake that there's an induction coming your way!

As has been the case with a lot of things that have gone before this point in the book, there are many and varied ways in which you may get your board induction (if you get one at all). Some companies may not offer it at all; others will do a 50/50 job of covering the bare necessities; the best experience will be from those companies that provide an integrated and comprehensive (though balanced and well-timed) induction program for you.

If you are getting very close to attending your first board meeting,

---

[19] www.brainyquote.com/quotes/authors/o/oscar_wilde_2.html

and it's all been a bit quiet on the board induction front, stick your hand up and enquire when it's coming. If it's not, then take stock from the following discussion points and ask your company to provide you with what you need either before your first meeting or not long afterwards.

Throughout a standard induction you'd expect to receive some reading materials. Hopefully, you will also be invited to the head office or operations centre to attend one or a number of meetings with the executives – possibly the CEO but definitely the company secretary – to go through the key areas that you need to be familiar with from day one.

The purpose of a board induction is several-fold:

- It can provide you with invaluable, ahead-of-the-game insights into the company's key safety, governance, risk, strategic, financial and operational structures; important frameworks (regulatory, safety, risk); delegations of authority protocols; public registers and policies.

- It provides you with the opportunity to meet staff and executives (who usually conduct the inductions), providing you with an early familiarity and an opportunity to build rapport with those you will be working with both inside and outside of the boardroom. You get the chance offline (so not in front of your board or chairman) to ask what you think might be some dumb questions. For your peace of mind, by the way, these are usually the best questions, being the ones that so many others want to ask but don't, for fear of how they'll look. I talk to this topic in greater detail later it the book. These questions could be about how the board works in practice, how the executives work together, anything you want to know about the company, its culture, strategy, etc.

- You get a chance to see how well the executives know the company and you'll get details of who can give you more information later if needed.

For very small companies, your induction may be with just one person and it could be your only chance before the first board meeting to ask any outstanding questions. If you only get to meet one person as part of your induction I'd recommend that it be the company secretary.

The company secretary

From my experience, the company secretary knows pretty much everything about what's going on in the company, including who's who in the zoo, the do's, the don'ts and everything in between. If the company secretary doesn't know the answer to any of your questions, he or she will know where to find it.

In larger companies, a meeting with the company secretary is an absolute must. For listed companies, this is particularly important due to the delicacies of sitting on these types of boards and the secretary will need to provide you with a number of information points to ensure you are fully informed from day one because they have a vested interest in keeping you out of 'breach territory'.

Matters that you will want to know about from the company secretary include:

1. **Conflict of interest:** What are the company's policies on conflicts of interest. A conflict of interest is when a clash arises between a person's duties to the company, or the interests of the company and its shareholders, and the person's interests or duties held to others outside of the company. Conflicts can be actual, potential or perceived, for example, where there's a perception that the person's role (be it an executive or director) cannot be implemented or carried out without the undue influence of the

outside interest or duty permeating across into their duties owed to the company.

You will also need to answer the following:

- What is the company's official definition of a conflict – are there examples you can be provided with?
- Is there a policy to read so that you never find yourself breaching these provisions?
- What types of interests do you have to declare on day one? These can include appointments on other boards, commercial or other arrangements, other roles or contracts that you have outside of this board which could infer an actual, potential or perceived conflict.

Get an understanding from the company secretary of what conflicts the company seeks to avoid and manage and how the management of conflicts works, both at and outside of board meetings (in terms of notification protocols, timings, etc.)

If it would provide you with more clarity and confidence, ask the company secretary to give you examples of what the company or its regulator would deem a conflict of interest, relative to the company concerned and your own commercial and personal circumstances.

2. **Director behaviour:** Are there any specific board policies or other inside tips to know regarding director behaviour when attending or responding to board meetings (e.g. codes of conduct, joining the meeting by means other than in person, leaving board meetings early, taking leave from the board, submitting proxies)?

3. **Attendance and absenteeism:** Are there specific policies on directors' attendance at meetings? (Note that a lot of publicly-listed and APRA-regulated institutions must publicly declare the

attendance records of directors on their websites – so if you don't go to your meetings, the whole world will see! – and if you are to eventually seek more board positions, this could hinder your ability to be considered for future board positions elsewhere.)

Can/should you appoint an alternate director? If so, how is it viewed by the board? (In some companies it is not provided for, but in others it's perfectly acceptable.) What if any restrictions exist? The constitution will also help you out on this one as that's primarily what will govern the board's management and use of alternate directors.

4. **Fit and proper process:** What would constitute a breach of the company's fit and proper processes – being found guilty of an offence, being a bankrupt, an adverse finding of a professional disciplinary body?

5. **Tenure provisions and caps:** Are there any tenure provisions, e.g. regarding being re-elected periodically, or tenure caps (you may see these noted in the constitution but they may also live in another governance policy).

6. **Directors' reviews:** Are the directors periodically reviewed for attendance and performance, and if so by whom? What happens with these reports? Who sees the content and how is it used?

7. **Disclosure obligations:** Is any other information required to be provided by you at any time in the future, e.g. if you buy certain shares or move house – what are your personal disclosure obligations (regardless of whether you are joining a listed or unlisted company)?

8. **Pending litigation:** Are there any current or expected major litigations or regulatory investigations afoot? (This would hopefully have come up in your pre-appointment checks.)

9. **Foreign interest:** If your company operates in foreign jurisdictions, are there any issues that you should know about as an incoming director that you may not have been privy to in your pre-appointment due diligence? What are the key elements of these foreign operations that are important to the board?

10. **Board minutes:** Now that you are a fully-fledged member of the board if you were unable to obtain a copy of them earlier, now is the time to ask to see a copy of the board's minutes from the past two to three years (or for the period you are comfortable asking for). The minutes (as we'll discuss in greater detail later on) are some of the most important records of a director's concern and reading past versions will give you a tremendous insight into the board's consideration of issues, how it oversees strategy and makes decisions on really important matters.

11. Finally, ask the company secretary whether the board sets down a minimum prescription for external training (in hours) to be completed annually to ensure or to support ongoing tenure of directors.

You should be able to leave your induction meeting with the company secretary with a clearer grasp of what the company expects and needs from its directors, and any particular industry-specific, operational or legal obligations that are attached to this board.

Committees and the committee chairman

More often than not, should the company's board have board committees as part of its governance structure, you are likely to end up on one of these at some point during your tenure (unless the company has a policy of you needing to have served for a certain period before this is contemplated).

If you know ahead of time or upon appointment that you will be appointed to a board committee, make sure you schedule a meeting in the diary of the committee chairman before your first committee meeting, or indeed before the company passes the requisite resolution to appoint you to the committee. This will ensure that you are somewhat advised of recent historical, current or material matters, as well as any other insights and basics that can set you up to be more productive in this role from the get-go.

Ensure that you obtain a copy of the committee's charter and, if you feel that it would help you to get a faster and more effective grasp on committee history, request that the executives appointed to oversee the committee provide you with requisite information before your first meeting. Other steps to take would be:

- Request a copy of the minutes from at least the past 12 months (or more) of committee meetings, to give you a flavour of the key matters which have come under their consideration. (If the committee only meets once or twice a year due to its nature, then extend out the review period.)

- You will also want to understand how that committee reports to the board on its activities and decisions; who is the governance adviser to it (the company secretary or other?); and what is its calendar of activities for the coming year or beyond?

- Check whether your appointment to this particular committee requires you to undertake further studies, training or courses in order to close any (potential) experience or information gaps you have, relative to the committee's mandate.

- For your development, the company should allow you to observe some of the board's committee meetings, even if you are not a member of them.

If you are provided with this opportunity definitely take it up (and take it up early in your tenure). If it's not offered, ask to have this arranged for you, particularly at the committees which cover audit, risk, finance, operations, strategy, products, consumers, etc. (there may be some sensitivity or questions of relevance for you to attend a remuneration or nominations committee depending on the company concerned).

Seeking out this experience not only demonstrates a tremendous interest by you in the workings of the board and the company, but more importantly it provides you with a direct insight into the matters being considered by the directors who sit on those committees (noting that you are part of the board which delegates part of its authority and responsibilities to these people).

It will broaden your understanding of the complexities or intricacies of the company and the industry in which it operates. Set this up with the committee chairman and the secretariat so that you can receive a copy of the committee's information pack ahead of the meeting date and ensure that a courtesy notification has been given to the committee chairman and/or other directors that you will be attending.

Remember to factor in more diary time and a personal level of additional commitment for pre-reading, travel, attendance, training and committee meetings when considering accepting a committee appointment.

7

MEETINGS: SCHEDULES AND PACKS

THE COMMITTED DIRECTOR will be super organised and plan their time well in advance. The time commitment involved when you become a first-time director can come as quite a surprise, so you need to schedule it as far in advance as possible.

Generally, the board or its secretariat will (or should) commence planning their next year's board dates well in advance to allow all directors to efficiently manage their diaries and commitments. It's in the company's interest to have you attend the maximum number of meetings possible, so be responsive to and engaged with this process.

ASX-listed and large corporate groups will potentially plan their board dates years in advance due to the nuances which come with:

- Having to work around directors who have multiple board appointments
- Boards which need to meet in various locations (domestically and potentially internationally)
- Having the experience to get in first, before any other company secretariat, to get the best dates before everyone else!

So don't be surprised if you are being asked what you are doing with your life two to three years out.

Scheduling meetings

Smaller boards may be happy with planning their dates annually, four to six months prior to the commencement of their new year. Smaller or family boards can often be far more malleable in moving dates around should a number of directors find they suddenly have meeting clashes.

When you receive the draft dates for board and board committee meetings from your secretariat ensure that you either pass them through to your PA for checking, or if managing your own diary you actually check the proposed dates against those already in your calendar. Don't forget to also check with your spouse or partner and across any other pre-planned or paid-for educational or conference events that are absolutely non-negotiable for you to attend during the subject period.

If you have clashes, let the secretariat (or in smaller companies your chair or fellow directors) know as soon as possible. If done early on in the process it provides the opportunity for them to make requisite changes (typically the secretariat will work backwards from the board or committee chairman's diaries).

Don't lob in late when responding to board date arrangements. Be a team player and follow the secretary's instructions regarding submitting your response on the proposed calendar.

If you have any other issues with the calendar definitely speak up during the review process – the directors should always get the chance to view the proposed meeting dates before they are submitted to the board for approval.

Long periods of absence

If you know you are going to be overseas, travelling or unavailable for an extended period of time during any calendar year, you will need to immediately inform both your chairman and the secretariat so everyone can work through options. These might include the appropriateness of you appointing an alternate director to sit in your seat while you are away (if this is permitted by the company's constitution). This will require board approval and due consideration prior to the application going in (as the alternate director will be subject to all the same approval processes you were during your appointment – so it's not to be taken lightly).

Appointing an alternate director for extended absences is a pragmatic approach for the company to ensure the board's operations are not jeopardised or unreasonably disrupted. But they do require a lot of work for all concerned, so there has to be a pretty good reason for them to do it. If it's due to a serious illness that will require you to take time away from all professional activities but your prognosis to return to professional duties is not in question, then definitely work it through with the company.

Remember you have significant and responsible duties to the company and its shareholders and stakeholders, so if you can't be there to do the role on an extended basis then take proactive action to address that. Your alternate director (unless prohibited by your constitution) can usually do all the things that you can do as a director unless you direct or restrict them in writing otherwise. Your company secretary will guide you through the due process here.

> **WARNING:** *If it's too long an absence period that you are proposing, then you may find the chairman discussing whether – on balance and with regard to everyone's interests – your tenure should continue.*

The company's and board's interests must come first. Your ego must run second here.

Reading your meeting packs

Anyone who knows me well in the secretariat space knows that this is one of my hobby horses (and indeed that of other secretariats and boards). The directors we love the most are those who read their packs well before a board or committee meeting – every time – not on the train the morning of, or in the cab on the way in from the airport with 30 minutes to go before kick-off time. The director who diligently schedules in sufficient pre-meeting reading time is the one who always wins the prize. Why? Well…it's your job. And the law requires you do this (not to mention all those stakeholders who are impacted by the decisions taken by your board).

"The key is not to prioritise your schedule, but to schedule your priorities." Stephen Covey[20]

Reading your pack before the meeting is non-negotiable. Not reading it before the meeting is unacceptable to your fellow directors, the regulations and the law.

Let's be clear here, the law requires you without exception to read every bit of your board pack – not every second word or to skim every paper, but to read everything. This goes to the care and diligence legal obligation discussed later in the book (s180 *Corporations Act*).

When you are setting up to start reading board packs, you will need to develop a game plan. This sounds a bit mundane but you should try and find a rhythm or some sort of regular approach to how you do this for your meetings. This allows you to maximise your time efficiently when board meeting packs arrive in your mail box or board portal. You can take advice or guidance from your fellow directors or from a mentor on how they approach reading their board packs. What I'm talking about here is working backwards from the meeting to

---

[20] www.brainyquote.com/quotes/quotes/s/stephencov133504.html

when you are likely to receive your board pack, then determining when and where you'll read it, how   much time will be required and how you'll make annotations, etc.

What the pack will include

The board pack will contain items such as:

- The agenda
- Previous meeting's minutes
- Potentially other types of formalities (maybe a gifts or conflicts register, other registers regarding the company's shareholdings or charges raised, director declarations on conflicts)
- An action tracker (tracking all previous actions that the board requested a report back on from management or others)
- Perhaps some updated financials or other budgetary reports (this is wholly bespoke to each company)
- Operational, risk, strategy, legal or other reports (the number and type of 'other' reports is obviously infinite and depends on the type and size of company you are joining)
- The CEO's report
- Sometimes chairmen submit their own report which may contain information on the latest governance matters regarding the company
- Papers from management requesting the board's noting or approval of X, Y and Z.

A really well-structured and professional meeting pack will always contain either a cover sheet or a self-contained instruction area for directors to read for every paper. This provides you with clarity on what management is requesting from the board in each paper (is the paper for approval, noting or endorsement?). You should know right from the start of your reading of the paper why the paper is in the board pack and what you are being asked to do.

It may be that the matter is something that only the board can approve. It could also be a board-owned and approved policy and as such, the only party authorised to amend it is the board.

The paper could be about a subject where the authority or power to approve it (or change it) cannot be delegated to management or even a board committee, e.g. the approval of the financials.

So hopefully for your sake you get a board pack which is well structured and put together, is clearly delineated from paper to paper, and has clear instructions attached to each paper on what management is seeking.

It's always a grand blessing as a director to receive really good quality board packs, as it will make the experience so much better than receiving poorly constructed and difficult to read ones.

There are boards that have insisted that individual papers are no more than two to three pages long. If they don't meet the criteria, the paper gets thrown out (that's code for it doesn't even make it into the pack). This works incredibly well where management can deliver on these instructions, and the chairman and CEO provide unwavering support to the company secretary to enforce it. It's generally a more delicate dance than this, but it's always fun considering how different boards approach this issue. Sometimes it can take years to settle on a balance that works for everyone.

Delivery and presentation of the pack

So here's where it gets interesting: as directors, you have an explicit role in determining how papers are delivered to you for your meetings. You will need to enquire with your secretariat as to how they distribute board papers for each meeting. Is it by delivery of a hard copy pack to your office or residence, via a dedicated online internet-based board portal, or via Dropbox (an internet-based document storage portal that is used by the public to share and send documents to other people

– access is via a link that is generated by the posting). Be sure to check this so you know by what method you will receive your meeting packs.

The board must confirm their needs and expectations with management as to how their papers are to be presented, otherwise, unless you have an unbelievably skilled and experienced management and secretariat team that absolutely nails the production of board papers every time (and acutely taps into directors' requests) you could end up with an encyclopaedia of material to read for every meeting.

Preparing highly informative board papers that are not books unto themselves is a skill that requires very strong executive engagement, such as by a CEO and chairman who won't accept standards anything less than that set by the board, and a company secretary who is duly authorised to reject papers that just don't meet the requisite standard. The combination of these elements makes for a dreamier board experience but it's less common than it should be.

The highest quality meeting papers are those which are skilfully honed, informative and provide the board with a balance of succinct and intelligent details such that the directors' ability to make considered decisions is at the highest level.

This is a whole-of-board issue – it's not your fight to have singularly. The golden rule I'm sharing with you is that you have to read every paper that is given to you – no matter how large it is – so if the pack form and content isn't working for you or your colleagues, you are compelled to raise this with the CEO or your chairman.

I've seen directors pick out questions on, e.g. page 63, section A, division i. of matter 2C of a 250 page meeting pack. That's how precisely they've read the papers and it's very impressive – not for the fact that they've climbed the Everest of a meeting pack and lived to tell the tale, but because they've done their job.

I've also seen instances where during discussions of a particular paper, management instantly knows from cues delivered by directors that the paper hasn't been read (or read very well).

Reading your papers well prior to the meeting also gives you an opportunity to ask questions of the CEO or executives (or author of the paper) before the meeting, about a certain matter you are unsure of or which you'd like further clarity on. Then during question time at the meeting, you can share with your fellow directors that you've spoken to ABC about XYZ prior to the meeting, and this was the outcome. This not only demonstrates your acute interest in the detail of the papers and the subject matter, but it also provides a learning point to share with your board, assisting with the decision-making for that item. Depending on what it is, it can also dramatically speed up board deliberations on matters that are better addressed at a level of detail outside the boardroom.

We're all human...

It's an absolute reality that at some point in your tenure (and probably more than once) human error will rear its head in the content of your board packs; it happens. And it will happen until the end of time. While all company secretaries and executive groups want their boards to have the very best quality and accurate information at every meeting, from time to time you will see an error in your materials.

The point of this section is to ask you to please not make it your only contribution as part of a multi-hour board meeting to call it out in front of the residual board. If management already knows about the error they will likely note it upfront as part of their presentation of the paper.

If it's not significant to the decision but notable in some other way, they will usually still appreciate you sharing your finding with them at the meeting break or at another suitable time.

Unless however it's really of significance to the decision being made, try and see an error for what it is. If you feel as though you do need to check the information before the meeting, given that it may affect the decision being made, absolutely don't hesitate to contact the executive or the author concerned (presuming this is allowable within the rules of your board). If you are unsure of the protocol here, give the company secretary a call at the time of finding the omission or error.

Taking care of your meeting pack

The papers in your meeting pack will be commercially-sensitive and are an important asset of the company. The safety and security of these records in your care is absolutely paramount. Wherever you keep them outside of the meeting, it is your job to keep them in a safe and secure place – not on the kitchen bench so that all and sundry can have a great Sunday read of them, nor in an unlocked back garden shed accessible to any prowling stalker or tradie passing by.

If you insist on retaining your physical board pack (which you don't have to do, as the company will always have its own copy) then you must take proactive and careful steps on how to house these documents. My preferred option is for directors to always hand the papers back to the company secretary at the end of the meeting so they can take care of them properly and in accordance with the company's document management policy. If they don't have a document management policy prescribing this, you can still hand them back in any case, and it will be the company's responsibility to take care of their disposal.

If you have them stored electronically, take advice from the secretariat on how these can be removed from your device after every meeting (if that's your preference or the company's policy to do so). Otherwise, how does the company approach keeping electronic documents safe? Does the secretariat or their IT department wipe these records by distance after a certain time has lapsed after the meeting?

You can keep and take with you any personal diary notes you've made during the meeting (be they recorded on a tablet or in writing, on the board papers or your own resources). However, these also need to be retained and safely secured. I discuss the legal implications of retaining these notes later.

Similarly, if you transport and keep your papers on an iPad, then the safety of that device needs to be a very high priority. Also take considerable care if your iPad is a shared resource in your family – it's not appropriate that little Susie, your partner or nanny are able to download your papers and have a great sticky-beak into what's going on at ABC Ltd.

If you have any questions or concerns about the safe-keeping of your papers – either upon receipt or regarding storage post the meeting – make it a point to contact the company secretary to discuss.

Minutes

One of the most important documents you'll ever read in your director's career will be the minutes of board meetings. There is a vast amount of articles and cases available for you to reference this very fact and one of the most famous recent cases on this topic was James Hardie.

Before I get to the James Hardie case, here are a few things to know about the minutes:

1. Minutes must be taken of every meeting of the directors to record the resolutions taken by the board and explain how they reached those decisions (be it a board or board committee meeting, or if the directors met by circular resolution i.e. with no physical meeting).[21]

2. Section 1308(2)[22] of the *Corporations Act* "…makes it an offence to make a statement in a document…which is false and misleading…Company minutes are such documents. Section

---

[21] www.austlii.edu.au/cgi-bin/sinodisp/au/legis/cth/consol_act/ca2001172/s251a.html?stem=0&synonyms=0&query=minutes; accessed 4th October 2014

[22] www.companydirectors.com.au/Director-Resource-Centre/Director-QA/Board-Meetings/Minutes-of-Directors-Meetings; accessed 4th October 2014

1308(4) makes it an offence for the directors…not to take all reasonable steps to ensure that a statement in such a document is not false and misleading[23]".

3. Once approved, the minutes of the directors' meeting are considered to be the most accurate and contemporaneous record of the decisions and activities undertaken at the meeting, unless evidence proves otherwise. What this generally means is that what's in the minutes is considered by the law and the courts to be that which occurred at that meeting.

If there are inaccuracies in the minutes, the time to raise these is when the minutes are being circulated to you in draft (usually by the company secretary) after the meeting, and definitely before you get your next meeting pack.

The reason being is that aside from the non-negotiable fact that the minutes are an accurate and true reflection of what happened at a meeting, the company secretary will also want to ensure that the draft is updated as quickly as possible with any material corrections, and ensure that they go into the next meeting pack with the greatest chance of being approved (for the efficiency of the board).

> **WARNING:** *It is critical that you read the minutes carefully and thoroughly every time. You can't approve them and then dispute their contents later in court when it doesn't suit.*

If you happen to discover an error in the minutes at the time of receiving your next meeting pack, but you had overlooked or missed it during the circulation of the draft minutes, don't worry (it's still a good thing!). But you must let the company secretary know as soon

---

[23] www.companydirectors.com.au/Director-Resource-Centre/Publications/The-Boardroom-Report/ Back-Volumes/Volume-12-2014/Volume-12-Issue-11/Important-reminders-from-the-courts; accessed 4th October 2014

as possible before the next meeting, so that arrangements can be made for the error to be noted to the board (and duly corrected) at the time the minutes are formally approved.

As per earlier statements, it is an offence to knowingly let inaccuracies stand in the minutes (being official *Corporations Act* documents), so don't ever be afraid to speak up if you think there are errors or misstatements in this document.

The issue with the James Hardie case was that the board approved a set of minutes from a particular meeting, but then sought to later say that what was in those minutes was inaccurate. Well, that's not how it works unfortunately. Some directors on that board 'fessed up that they hadn't even read their minutes. Given the incredible importance of the minutes and how this document can turn a court decision against your favour, it is in your interests and those of your stakeholders to always read your minutes very carefully.

Here's a colourful expression of this necessity for your thoughts:

> "...*a contemporaneous written record of a meeting, particularly something official like minutes, is evidence of the truth of what it says, and will trump other evidence which is really just inference... It's a simple truth that whoever drafts the minutes is king, and directors would always be well advised to actually read the draft minutes before they blithely approve them at their next meeting. They will be forever stuck with whatever the minutes say.*"[24]

A quick reminder: if you were absent for the whole or part of a board or board committee meeting, be sure to obtain a copy of the draft minutes of that meeting once completed, to ensure you remain up to date on key activities and decisions made and to provide you with an opportunity to canvas or flesh out any decisions made at the meeting with the chairman, CEO or executives.

---

[24] www.mondaq.com/australia/x/176308/Directors+Officers+Executives+Shareholders/
High+Court+gives+James+Hardie+directors+the+shove; accessed 4th October 2014

8

THE DO'S AND DON'TS OF BOARD BEHAVIOUR

YOU HAVE NOW been appointed and it's time for you to turn up and sit at the board table with the rest of your director colleagues. This is what you've been aiming for, having done all of that due diligence and then been duly appointed to the board. Effectively, that's been your pre-season; now you get to go to the game and that's where the fun really starts!

Putting aside this sporting analogy, directorship is anything but a game; it's a serious and responsible appointment with due consequence (for you and your stakeholders). Your board and committee meetings are not just another appointment in your diary where you have to turn up and pretend you're interested.

Board meetings are where so many of the biggest and most material decisions in a company are taken. The behaviours, decisions and actions (or inaction) taken at board meetings can be the catalysts of new corporate governance laws enacted by our legislators or regulators. The board meeting is the place where decisions taken can impact the lives of many, many people. That's why it's a privilege to sit on a board.

That's why the average Joe who doesn't have the requisite commitment to do this job properly, shouldn't be on a board.

Sometimes, board meetings can throw up the most tremendously insightful learning experiences. This will depend on the type of company you join and the quality of the directors sitting around the table with you. The experience of being a director cannot be catalogued or defined in one tight sentence, it's each to their own and your takeaways from the appointment will always be slightly different than anyone else's.

So if you are brand new in this space and have just secured your first appointment, you are now ready to walk into this boardroom for the first time and it's best I give you some hints and tips on this.

Take heart, everyone who's an experienced director knows exactly what it's like to step into their very first boardroom.

Even the greatest directors in the country had to start somewhere, they all had a first board meeting.

It will be decidedly different sitting as a director at the board table than it ever was as an executive. It just is, and you should expect it to be. Embrace this challenge; embrace the uncertainty, the future learnings, all that's coming towards you, all of the insights, discussions and opportunities for growth. The opportunity to be exposed to a variety of education points, options, alternatives and strategy-setting will hopefully prove an invigorating and stimulating experience.

Now I can't say or guarantee that every board or committee meeting you will ever attend in your life as a director will leave you inspired and educated; that would be a major fib. However, it's rare that I've ever attended a board or committee meeting where I haven't learned at least one new thing. That's a great gift and it's why I love this element of my work. The reality of the minute-taker is that by the time they get to do the minutes of the meeting they've actually lived the details three times over – once in preparing the meeting papers, then sitting through the actual meeting, followed by doing the minutes. So it's like watching the same movie three times over. Lucky for you as a director, you only have to live it out twice!

There are things that I've seen and learned at board meetings that I take everywhere with me in my professional and personal capacity. These are both functional business facts and experiences (regarding how businesses are actually run and all of the elements involved therein). But importantly, also, are how people's behaviours as a group impact the organisation's culture, leadership and ability to deliver on what's promised and expected.

The boardroom should not be a zoo, a free-for-all society or a totally stifled or dictatorial experience. What it should be is a democratic, collegiate (this is not code for 'group think' – see glossary at the back of the book) and a respectful coming together of a group of aligned people who are committed to the cause of the company and its stakeholders.

So I hope you do find yourself among quality, talented and committed individuals who are there for all the right reasons. Otherwise you'll be in for all sorts of new and unexpected experiences that you can describe as a bonus or otherwise!

Your very first meeting

Remember, despite having conducted thorough due diligence and taken part (hopefully) in your board induction, you are not automatically expected to go into your first board meeting knowing every single thing about every policy, strategy and operational matter of the company.

Building a knowledge-base on the company as a director takes years so don't feel any pressure to be the A-grade student on day one – it doesn't work that way.

You've now arrived at the office and you're walking into the boardroom. If you are generally a nervous person, then this will be a minute-by-minute proposition for you. Don't put any more pressure on yourself than to get from one minute to the next. Nothing bad will happen to you at your first meeting. However, this is your last zero expectation day where no-one really expects much from you at all. Take it all in. Enjoy it.

If you are the ultra-prepared kind, or take comfort from being well-researched before undertaking new experiences, what you can do (say a few days or the night before) is re-visit the photos of the board and the executives on the internet (if you are lucky to have these) and refresh on people's backgrounds and faces. You don't need to rote-learn this, it's just so that you can recognise a couple of people when you arrive. If you've had a board induction program prior to your first meeting then obviously you'll have met some executives who may be milling around the boardroom just before kick-off – so you'll likely see some familiar faces in that case.

Also check and double-check that you know where the meeting is being held and the start time.

Everyone will know upon your arrival that you are the new director. They've been expecting you – enjoy the introductions and being the new kid. Depending on your corporate experience in boardrooms, you may feel completely at home and at ease on this your first day, or you may feel like you've just landed on another planet.

The first meeting obviously carries everything with it in being brand new, so get through it and you'll feel so much more comfortable next time around. It's like reading the board pack of a new company for the very first time. Things will be presented to you in unfamiliar templates and structures; it may make you nervous even just reading your first meeting pack. But take it a step and a meeting at a time. You'll get used to the routine and the faces very quickly.

Make sure you greet the chairman and CEO as soon as you can after arriving and ensure the company secretary or supervising governance practitioner knows you are there (they may be your reception contact anyway). Choose a seat, put your things down and you'll be off and running.

✔ TIPS FOR THE ROOKIES

☐ **Don't sit next to the chairman of the meeting.** This is the case not only for your first day but potentially (company depending) for each meeting thereafter. This spot may be reserved for the CEO but it will almost certainly be where the company secretary or minute-taker wants to sit. (This is because the company secretary, governance practitioner/ minute-taker needs to be able to communicate and send messages to the chair during the meeting, e.g. if they need the chairman to go faster or slower in directing the meeting; if someone's not turned up, or if there is some other glitch or technicality that they need to quietly and seamlessly inform their chairman of – they can't do this from the other end of the boardroom table, so anticipate that they'll have dibs on the seat next to the chairman.)

☐ **Don't worry if you are asked to move chairs.** If someone moves you on from where you've plonked down your things don't feel like a ninny or be offended – there may be a pre-ascribed seating arrangement you weren't informed about. Or quite simply someone needs to be near the overhead projector or have easy access to do a phone dial in. I've had times where I've had to ask the chairman of a board to please move to another seat so that I could be next to the meeting chairman. People get it, so don't take it personally if that's the seat you accidentally find yourself in.

☐ **Graciously accept the chairman's introduction of you as a new director.** The chairman will (hopefully!) publicly

---

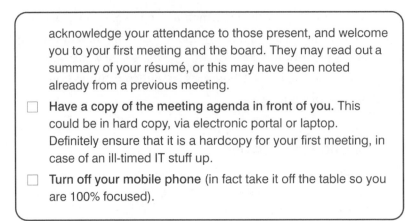

acknowledge your attendance to those present, and welcome you to your first meeting and the board. They may read out a summary of your résumé, or this may have been noted already from a previous meeting.

☐ **Have a copy of the meeting agenda in front of you.** This could be in hard copy, via electronic portal or laptop. Definitely ensure that it is a hardcopy for your first meeting, in case of an ill-timed IT stuff up.

☐ **Turn off your mobile phone** (in fact take it off the table so you are 100% focused).

The joy of the first meeting is that even though you need to be highly prepared (to the standard discussed earlier as you may need to vote on a matter) no-one truly expects you to say or contribute anything of considerable substance at your very first meeting… unless you've found yourself in a first meeting where there's a crisis afoot or a massive decision to be made, and everyone's vote at the table will count towards a significant resolution in the life of the company (highly unusual but it could happen). If that is the case then make sure you get extra prepping prior to the meeting and have necessary discussions with the CEO or relevant executive beforehand to be fully briefed on this matter. Your vote counts equally, even if it is your first meeting, so ensure you're comfortable with where you've landed here.

Watch and learn

I've rarely seen a director required to contribute anything of material significance verbally at their very first board meeting – regardless of the size or status of the company. For people's first meetings (and especially for first-time directors) I know of no person who leaves the room and complains that you were silent the whole time. If they do, then they haven't been around the block very often or been in too many boardrooms. The board wants you to take your time to reflect and consider how the board's dynamics work and to understand the routines and approaches taken; to build on your knowledge of the company and the industry.

This will allow you to grow into a more effective and reflective director over time. No-one wants a know-it-all director at the table for their first meeting, nor (in reality) do they want you asking a plethora of questions that you really should be taking offline with the CEO or the executives first. For most boards, this is the meeting to be contemplative.

That's not to say that you absolutely can't speak or reflect on an issue that's under discussion – you are not bound and gagged and prohibited from speaking just because it's your first meeting. It's just saying that there's no secret or other onerous expectation on you to do so.

The best thing you can do is to take it all in and observe. How does the chairman chair the meeting? You can now see their style in practice and what to expect at future meetings. Also take in the dynamics in the room:

- Where are the other directors sitting (who's paired up with who)?
- What other people attend the meeting (e.g. executives, company secretary, management, consultants, auditors)?
- How does the conversation flow?
- Do you see the directors engaging in each agenda item with active and energetic discussion, or is it clear that some items pique their attention more than others?
- Is there any obvious group think at work?
- Were there agenda items which they really got stuck on and had difficulty making a decision about? If yes, why do you think that was so? Was it due to the complexity of the issue, its history

perhaps, or was it because there were clear divides of opinion around the table on the options available to the company?

Your first meeting is a fantastic opportunity to absorb the boardroom in session.

Now, it could be that the agenda for your first meeting is incredibly vanilla and there's really not much doing on that occasion. So you may feel a bit duped that you haven't been able to see a lot more of the board in action on something meaty (and thus observe how the directors perform under a bit of pressure). But this is still a fantastic opportunity for observation – any which way the agenda falls. The meatier and pressured meetings will eventually come!

Observe also whether any of the directors are doing things which annoy or cause the other directors (or executives) to become agitated (and therefore perhaps you can file these observations as things not to do to your fellow colleagues):

- Is there someone there who looks like they are going to be difficult to work with?
- Is there a particular director who really puts management through the wringer regarding the paper they've put forward?
- How hard does the board press management on what's being proposed?
- Is there someone who appears to dominate each and every conversation, or conversely is very quiet and reflective?

Board stereotypes

During your journey as a company director you will come across the most interesting, amusing, well-educated, insightful, frustrating, ferocious, precocious, demanding, silent, soft and amazing types of board colleagues.

There are as many types of directors in this world as there are in the encyclopaedia of personalities, and it's actually good fun – if nothing else – to see them going for it with all their gusto! As mentioned earlier, being privy to all forms of board diversity is a gift and one that you can take a tremendous amount from throughout your journey – not only as a director, but also in your professional and personal life.

It is good, however, to be aware ahead of time just how different people can be around the board table, and it will be interesting to see how many of these 'types' you come across in your board career. Here's just a sample of the ones that exist (as observed through my own eyes or through tales of the table). This list is not based on even one iota of science or research – just years of sitting at board tables and taking in the view. I wonder...which one will you be?

- The worry wart
- The devil's advocate
- The uninformed and lazy director
- The impatient director
- The deliberator
- The she'll be right director
- The risk averse
- The options lover
- The copycat
- The pioneer
- The unconstructive, argumentative director
- The opaque director
- The acceptor
- The police officer
- The constant voice
- The late lobber
- The pedantic one

The worry wart

This person can be a bit of hard work, and you do want to keep them reasonably calm and very well-informed. A (perceived) lack of information or uncertainty can make them most uncomfortable and potentially destabilise their capacity for considered decision-making. You also only want one of these on your board (max) so we'll assume that if they are there, they have tremendous other skills to contribute.

The good thing about worry warts is they can make the board think about risks and may be more comfortable than others in delaying a decision. The value of the worry wart comes down to the context of the situation. They can be a beacon of rationality and learned patience, but can also be a slight impediment to balanced commercial decision-making. The thing with the worry wart is that you should at least hear what is bugging them and then determine whether that's been mitigated already, or whether they are actually breaking new ground.

The devil's advocate

This personality is one of my favourites because they are the directors who are prepared to stick their necks out and challenge what's being presented, to dig deeper and go further than others. Or at least they challenge what's being presented to them. These directors are happy to push management's position just a little bit further than others, and are usually very genuine in their desire to get a duly informed and considered decision or outcome for the company. I think they are a great asset to boards who are strongly collegiate and who – without this type of director – would never disagree or push the edges on any important matter. Especially for shareholders, these guys – when they perform constructively – can be really good for your business.

The uninformed and lazy director

Those who don't read their papers, continually miss board meetings, ask clearly uninformed questions or consistently under-contribute. You have to ask yourself why they bother continuing to turn up – perhaps the catering's too good, the pre-meeting dinner is fabulous or it's just plain good business for their CV to have your company listed on it. They should do the world a favour and resign, putting their lack of commitment to use somewhere else. They infuriate their fellow directors, are disappointing to whoever nominated them, they don't help to build confidence in the board, and they have no value-add for shareholders or management.

The impatient director

('…can it just be over already?' '…a quick game is a good game…'). These people will let you (and sometimes the chairman) know when their patience is up – either on a single matter, a line of questioning or the entire meeting. Disruptive behaviour is their call sign. They might start a loud, distracting or very long side-conversation with their neighbour (while others are speaking or presenting papers), start reading the newspaper (sad but true), write their shopping or to-do lists rather indiscreetly, log into (and send) emails, or just leave the room entirely. I've also seen people fold their arms, lean back and look to the heavens praying for it to be over.

Sometimes they move their papers around very loudly, bow their head or outwardly suggest via various body language that the matter has been sufficiently dealt with and that everyone should just move along (it doesn't matter that that's the chairman's job).

They can be difficult directors at times because when it counts, matters do warrant an in-depth or multiple-event discussion due to their complexity or risk. So it's important that the impatient director is not given the opportunity to simply make the decision for the whole board or the chairman or to overly influence the pace of decision-making. These types pose an interesting personality challenge for directors and the chairman alike.

The deliberator

('…hmmm') Potentially a hybrid of the worry wart, the considered director and the devil's advocate. They really don't like making one-sided or quick decisions, and will struggle sometimes if only one option is put on the table. They really do like to (often outwardly) weigh up all options, debate and trade off the pros and cons of the decision or opportunity. It's great to have directors who wish to contemplate the key angles of a matter but not so much that they end up becoming a stranglehold of the board's ability to make decisions efficiently.

The she'll-be-right director

('…we've discussed it for a while now and there are plenty of assets behind us – what's the worst thing that could happen?'). This type of director can be seen as a little more 'cruisy' or relaxed about the eventual possible outcomes of decision-making. Or perhaps they are always like this in their other commercial dealings outside of the board and it's worked well for them so far – it's just how they are built. They don't necessarily need an over-abundance of discussion (beyond a certain level) to get to what might be the same conclusion anyway. They are quick (in their own minds) to balance out the risk and opportunity and come to a decision.

The really risk-averse

A tip to the risk averse director – a company can't make money without taking risks…just saying… Well this one's a little troublesome I have to warn you. How did they have the courage to take the plunge and sign their Consent to Act in the first place, given the risks attached to directorship? Or perhaps they have an unrivalled insurance policy behind them! The risk-averse director can prove difficult for their board colleagues and management around decision-making. Quite possibly you could not provide this type of director with enough comfort or information to ever make them happy. I hope for the sake of your board that the chairman does not let too many (if any) of these types get onto the board in the first place because they can be very stifling for growing and dynamic companies (especially if the voting mechanism at the board requires a very high percentage to pass resolutions).

The options lover

'…but we haven't tested this yet in another 25 different ways…': another hybrid type – a bit deliberator and a bit devil's advocate perhaps. They like to know every detail about every option, what it means, whether it's been stress-tested. Giving them only one or two options would make them terribly nervous. Surely there must be more alternatives, they'll be quietly thinking. Has management really done its job here? Do we need external assistance or advice? We must have missed something perhaps?

These guys can drive everyone a bit batty if their behaviour is applied to every matter needing a decision. In saying this, they are a guard against void or quick decision-making, or a board dominated by group think. Again, a challenge for the chairman, and one that management needs to be alert to going into decision papers.

The copycat

The let's-check-and-see-what-everyone-else-on-the-planet-is-doing first director. Well you know…safety in numbers and if it worked for them, it will work for us. Copying makes them look like they are in tune with the market and the competition. Others will think of this type of director as stifling or lacking in risk appetite, and that the company should do what's best for itself and the shareholders for a change (and not what others in the same industry are doing or have done already).

There may be safety in numbers and a perceived value by these directors in copying the strategies or products of others, but being a mirror image of your competition can be a good long-term bet for disaster, a law suit even and non-sustainable results. There's perhaps a little of the risk-averse personality also at play here. While the chairman should always give respectful airtime to all directors' concerns and ideas, hopefully the board won't be too persuaded by this type of director even if they are strong-minded and argue convincingly.

The pioneer

Every initiative, opportunity or approach should be fresh and unique, first in the market, or they are happy to trial new technology or ideas – these are cracking directors to have on the board as they are comfortable with risk and greenfield opportunities, they understand the market in which they are playing and are comfortable with the prospect that sometimes things will fail (and that when they do, the company needs to fail fast and move on).

They want to push the company towards innovation, new thinking and competitive positioning. They are happy to push the boundaries of what's been done before in the company or the market. They tend to like a challenge and are not afraid of options and combinations of strategies to make something work.

The only downside is that they may always want to over-test the company, whereas sometimes (just sometimes) boards and companies may need to forgo being a pioneer or entirely innovative with something to achieve a better outcome. Not everything has to be a revolution. Generally, however, these are fantastic directors to work with, and a switched-on and highly engaged management team will really enjoy working with this personality type.

The unconstructive or argumentative director

Somewhere, at some time, someone has taken these people aside and told them that being argumentative is demonstrative of their capability as a director. In reality, they are just being disruptive, love to hear their own voice or are not recognising the difference between how one provides constructive feedback (or undertakes quality probing questioning) versus being a liability in the conversation. It's not to say that we shouldn't be encouraging lively debate and discussions at the board table – quite the contrary. However, there is a fine and learned line between being a strong contributor who really wants to flesh out the issues at hand and being a detractor. It's safe to say that being publicly known as a non-constructive arguer at the board table is not a sure-fire way of elevating or extending your board career.

The opaque director

(You can't read them for anything, or what they say can be construed in many different ways.) These are tricky personalities and sometimes their style can be identified through silence (as in, at most meetings) or it could be that their lines of questioning occur mostly outside of board meetings. They may also have a talent for asking questions at meetings which don't suggest which way they are leaning on a particular topic. The danger for the CEO and management with these directors is that you never know what you might be in for at the next meeting or where they might be heading with their position. They play a strategic though quiet role in the boardroom dynamic but don't underestimate them, as they can sometimes come out of left field (perhaps quite late in the piece) with a big left hook and knock you off your seat.

If you are a people-watcher like me, they keep the game interesting. Usually their questions are asked in a considered and well thought-through way. If yours is a board that actively votes on split matters, these are the directors that management will watch carefully.

The acceptor

Whatever management thinks is a good idea is good enough for them.

This type of director frequently lacks confidence and might not want to show that they are unsure of the matter at hand, or that they don't otherwise know the difference between the options being put forward. The chairman needs to have a dialogue with any 'acceptors' on the board, as their style can be a liability for the overall dynamics and capability required of the board. You need people who are willing and able to challenge, engage, query and debate items on the table – not just accept at management's word all being put before them. Otherwise what's the point? Where's the value-add in their appointment?

The police officer

This director gets a great deal of satisfaction (and therefore thinks they are doing their job brilliantly and extinguishing their director's duties at the same time) from picking on things that they believe management has, or hasn't done. They are looking for the errors, the oversights. It is rare that they offer praise and would never admit getting their own interpretations wrong. These are difficult directors to deal with. They unfortunately over-play their authority hand, confusing it with constructive assistance. You would hope your board is not a calling ground for this personality type as their presence will become wearisome very quickly.

The constant voice

The one who really needs to be heard on every agenda item. Take it from me, there's no rule book anywhere which says that to be a valued and contributing director you need to have your voice heard on every single agenda item at every meeting (there's no KPI for that).

No, in fact the most effective and valued directors are those who raise their hand when they genuinely have a constructive and learned point to make, or to ask an important or highly relevant question. They bide their time for an appropriate moment to speak and critically read the room and prior discussions to work out the lay of the land.

At the opposite end is the director who thinks just the reverse is the way to go and falls over themselves to be the greatest verbal contributor of them all. Now, if the chairman allows this behaviour to be exhibited on an ongoing basis, it might be that another director or the CEO makes comment accordingly. It's not necessarily that what they have to say is not well-received or of value. However, no-one judges anyone just because they don't speak up on every agenda item.

The late lobber

The one who always leaves it right until the last minute to call something out or require a new condition be added – having had many, many opportunities to do so earlier. Where have you been, we will all be asking silently and frustratingly? I'm not saying that you should stay quiet if something (material) genuinely bothers you and you've missed a better (earlier) time in which to make a call for further discussion. But otherwise, try to be in the moment when the board is considering the issues deeply, so that you're not seen as the eternal coat-dragger.

The pedantic one

If the details in the paper are perfect, then the board's decision will be complete. As a secretariat, we pick these guys early. They are usually extremely well-meaning and committed directors; however their need for absolute perfection in their board papers (or in other matters) can be a bit much relative to what's actually at stake.

The pedantic director will make you earn your stripes. They genuinely believe that absolute perfection of the written word is their gift to the board and the organisation. No-one will ever mind a director pointing out a material omission, error or misstatement in a paper. However, the director whose main contribution to the board is a constant correction of spelling or grammar errors is really not that impressive to anyone who's been in this game for more than five minutes.

I could go on, trust me, but let's move on – the point I'm making is that you will inevitably find yourself inside a boardroom with many different personality types, and it's both good fun and enlightening to be alert to what's driving certain behaviours or tendencies.

Diversity in all of its forms is incredibly healthy for boards, including the way in which people work through making decisions. Diversity in character, style and contributions will always be to the advantage of the board and the company on the proviso that while each person may apply their own tendencies and personal attributions to decision-making, at the end of the day what matters most is their collective ability to make well-considered decisions.

Watching a diverse and skilled director group go through their decision-making process at the board table is both educational and insightful – and usually produces learnings for all involved.

It's when your board gets bogged down on insignificant matters that things can become unstuck, or when they struggle to find common ground. As long as the board is putting the company's, shareholders or members' interests first (while also considering stakeholders) when making decisions that process generally has the greatest opportunity of working itself out going through to a conclusion. Having a skilled and respected chairman who can ably steer their board through bumpy decision-making will also go a long way towards achieving an outcome.

Private sessions

There is a practice undertaken by some boards where the non-executive directors meet (regularly or just when needed) without management or other non-board members being in the room. This includes the CEO, managing director and executive directors. This practice can be held at the start of a meeting or just before (or after) a really important agenda item. It is an interesting area of board practice. In working it into agendas on a recurring basis, it means that management knows it will occur at each meeting and it becomes an accepted and valued time component of a board's work program.

Essentially it's an opportunity for directors to discuss any manner of issues or concerns that they'd prefer not to initially discuss in front of the executive or management group. It may include discussions on legal issues, the CEO's performance, succession-planning or concerns with paper quality, information flows or other matters. There are no rules for this type of session and so it's totally bespoke as to what the directors want from it.

The sessions are chances for the board to have broad, unrestricted discussions on sometimes quite sensitive matters. Or the sessions can play a 'meeting of the minds' role to test where the board is at on a particular issue before taking it to management. It can be anything really. You might also observe and be party to the board or board committees having these sessions from time to time with the company's internal auditor (if there is one) and the external auditors. If you see something on your board meeting agenda called 'in-camera' or 'private session' this is what it will be. You need to be in that session – it's not code for you being able to skip it and just arrive in time for the first 'real' agenda item.

So we come to the end of your first meeting. Hopefully you will have found the experience incredibly insightful and it positions you for all those joyous meetings to come!

9

WHEN YOU CAN'T MAKE A MEETING

"Action expresses priorities."

GHANDI[25]

OK, SO YOU'VE attended your first board meeting, you've got a preliminary take on 'who's who in the zoo', plus taken in a few interesting observations. You're ready to get into things.

Despite all your best plans and intentions there may be an occasion/s when you just can't physically attend a board meeting or you need to be excused before it has ended. Let's have a look here at how to handle these situations.

As an exemplary director, you will be 100% aiming to get to every meeting that is scheduled for the duration of your tenure on any board. I love you for that already. However, life being what it is, even the most amazing, committed and gallant of directors may miss a meeting (OK then two) during their directorship career. Things will

---

[25] www.writechangegrow.com/2012/04/10-thought-provoking-lessons-from-mahatma-gandhi/; accessed 28 March 2015

happen in your personal life which require you to be somewhere else other than in that boardroom due to extraordinary or emergency circumstances. Let's discuss below how meeting absences can be handled and give you some do's and don'ts when this need arises.

Examples of what constitutes a qualifying reason for not joining a meeting in person for any period of the agenda include:

- You have had a death in the family (or there's one imminent), or you've had a direct family member rushed to hospital with a critical injury or illness – no questions asked; goes without saying

- You are on jury service

- You are appearing before a parliamentary committee hearing or senate enquiry (or similar) and there's no wriggle room date-wise for your attendance to be shifted

- You have a commitment to a life-significant overseas trip which was arranged months before you were even remotely being considered for this role, and so if (as an example) you attempted to dial into your company's board meeting from your Italian hillside villa on say your 20th wedding anniversary, you would soon be known as the 'newly single director' or the one looking for a great divorce lawyer

- You have a genuine need to be at home for an absolutely critical family matter and have no ability to properly join and contribute to the meeting by other means.

Obviously in emergency situations, where you absolutely can and where it's appropriate (given all circumstances) you must try to let the chairman, CEO or secretariat know of your unexpected absence as early as you can – if possible ring or send a text. If that's not possible then just concentrate on what you're doing and forget about the board meeting, ask someone else to call those just mentioned, or call or text halfway through. Everyone on your board is a human being so there will never be any ill-will exhibited should you find yourself subject to those circumstances noted above and therefore unable to make a board meeting without notice.

There are, however, plenty of other times when directors want to show up for the first part of a meeting and then leave thereafter, or are unable to come in person but can join remotely.

Being excused early

If you know before a particular meeting that you will need to be excused to leave early, you must let the company secretary and/or governance adviser know, as well as the chairman. This is not only an expected courtesy, but it also lets these parties know of your intended departure without surprise (and it can be worked into the chairman's run sheet or meeting instructions if used).

It also allows the secretary to check the agenda for the period of your absence to see whether there will be any approval items coming up that are either significant in nature, or which absolutely need your vote to be passed (or not). The secretary can then work with the chairman to potentially amend the agenda order (if it's non-negotiable that the whole board is in attendance for that portion of the meeting).

Critically, however, if leaving at a certain time leaves the board with no quorum, then you are withdrawing the board's ability to make decisions on possibly very important matters.

It's incredibly important that you give as much advanced notice as possible to the requisite parties if you need to leave early.

The best time to do this is the minute you become aware of it – preferably this would be well before the meeting pack gets distributed so the agenda can be ordered appropriately. If you only find out that you need to leave early after the pack has gone out, then immediately notify the secretariat and chairman so that arrangements can be made to either alter the agenda on the day, or to check whether a quorum will still be held at the time of your departure.

Always apologise (sounds basic but this can be a forgotten or overlooked step by some directors).

Absent of a phenomenal life-impacting excuse, telling the company secretary and the chairman on the morning of the meeting, or at morning tea that you have to leave during proceedings is a big no-no. Please don't do this – it's highly annoying and disappointing behaviour. We all understand that a personal crisis can arise either just before or even during a meeting that was 100% completely unforeseen (e.g. a family member has been taken to hospital) and no-one will ever have an issue with you leaving if this happens. However, qualifying instances of this type, i.e. leaving with little to zero notice to the board, are set aside for those with a very high human significance attached.

Another big no-no is leaving the board meeting to go to someone else's board meeting.

Curiously, it happens. Everyone understands that directors have a very busy portfolio of professional commitments, including roles on other boards. But really – are you serious? It should be both an unremarkable and unspoken expectation that directors must stay for the entire board meeting. If you are leaving the meeting to go to someone else's meeting it's a horrifically bad look and it will be frowned upon behind your back. Rude and non-sympathetic as it might sound, that's what will happen.

There are some hugely patient and tolerant chairmen who will not appear to have an (outward) problem with you doing this (and most directors can live with the private scourge of the company secretary that will accompany you leaving the meeting early to go to someone else's). However, when you get down to the real reason of why the board exists and to whom it owes its duties, it's a bit poor to cut and run half way (and sometimes a bit less) through the meeting. People may judge me harshly on this position, but it is an incredibly irksome practice that we really only support in the most deserving of circumstances.

Remote meeting attendance

Sometimes there may be reasons why you need to join the meeting from afar. If the constitution of the company and the board charter allow you to attend meetings other than in the flesh then you may be able to join the meeting by phone, Skype or video link. To do this you must tell the secretariat and/or the chairman as soon as you know you can't be there in person. The rules of your board may actually require you to seek prior permission to do this or there may be flow-on effects procedurally, so informing people upfront is important and a professional courtesy to the board.

Giving solid prior notice to the company secretary allows them to make appropriate arrangements with the IT department or board IT, or with telephones, so that there's every chance things run smoothly on the day.

When accommodating directors joining a board meeting by a means other than in person, I've had them do so when on the deck of a ship in the middle of the ocean (by satellite phone), in airport lounges (enjoying the continual stream of overhead announcements concerning departing flights when their phones were off mute), in dodgy foreign hotels, in the back of taxis, at home, in the park or in shopping centres. (Some of these are not ideal places from where to join a board meeting... just saying.)

It's really important that we know as far ahead as possible how the meeting set-up needs to be done and whether there can be a back-up plan should something go awry.

Giving prior notice of your remote attendance (if it's to be arranged) for any one meeting also allows the secretariat to communicate this to the executives or presenters, so that when they enter the room and are doing their presentations they know which directors are on the phone.

It's also incredibly important if there are tabled papers given out at the meeting. Knowing of your external connection allows for arrangements to be made beforehand to get you the papers in a timely fashion before decisions have to be made. This will provide for your informed participation in the meeting and will allow you to accurately follow the conversation and presentations.

Abstaining due to lack of papers

If there are papers given to directors attending in person which have not been distributed to you prior to joining the call (or on the call), and those papers are critical to the decision being made, you absolutely should not vote on that matter. You must confirm your abstention to the chairman at the time the paper is being tabled, if the decision that's in question can't be made without this new information.

The rule also extends to the situation even when you are there in person. If you have been given a paper during, or just prior to, a meeting (or even the current agenda item), and have not had the ability to properly read, review and reflect on what's being asked to be approved, if the decision is even remotely important then you absolutely should not vote on it. You must abstain and this must be noted in the minutes.

This was a noted issue in the James Hardie case and has been an area to watch known by company secretaries for a very long time. It's extremely poor form for an executive to email you a paper while you are online or on the phone for a board meeting, expecting you to be part of the approval with little to no prior notice. If your vote is important to the decision, or without it there is no quorum, the meeting should be adjourned for a suitable period of time for you to be able to read and digest the paper properly, before returning to a voting scenario.

> **CAUTION:** *As part of that board, you will be held accountable for the decision so never be pushed into voting on a matter which you just haven't been given proper and prior notice of.*

This is just one of those cases where you have to be brave and hold out on what's the right thing to do. People can get on a roll in meetings when they just go along with things and then half-way through realise that they really shouldn't be doing this or that. If for some reason the chairman or the secretariat hasn't realised that you shouldn't be voting on the paper, or that you and others need time out to read the paper, you are just going to have to suck up your embarrassment and call it out. It's just too important not to do so.

Joining a meeting remotely but not by phone

While it's tolerated to differing degrees (every board's appetite for this is different), boards can struggle with conducting meetings by telephone or other non-visual means. There are some brilliant visual communication tools now available that boards are starting to use, particularly those with global operations and where directors are based in other countries.

The reason why the non-visual tools are not favoured is because the chairman can't as easily see what your body language is or how the board dynamic is faring on any part of the agenda. This is a vital piece of information for a chairman who needs to be able to 'read the room' as part of their effective chairing of the meeting. People are usually pretty clear (though often unconscious) communicators with their bodies, including folding their arms, moving their eyes a certain way, moving their lips into certain shapes. Depending on whether they can see you or not, it can be difficult for the chairman to gauge your interest in a particular discussion when you are not physically in the room.

Without the benefit of body language, the chairman has reduced their ability to conduct a good meeting for the benefit of all directors. So it is a loss to the board in some way if you are not there in person. Great chairmen will absolutely ensure that everyone on the phone is always accounted for – contribution-wise – in every agenda item, and is introduced each time a new presenter comes to the table (the company secretary may give the chairman a reminding prod but it's all coming from the same good place).

> *Just another tip – if you are joining a meeting by externally-hosted visual means, it's always a good move to stay awake for the whole meeting – obvious though that may seem!*

Watch for this, especially if you are joining a board meeting being held in another hemisphere in the middle of the night or early morning, and you've just not had your quota of sleep (or perhaps you've had a little too much or not enough of something else!).

This banging on about not being at meetings in person is not so much to give you a hard time and therefore shame you into never doing it, but just don't do it regularly, especially if it goes against the board's own attendance policies.

You may be joining a board which totally does not expect to see you in person at meetings for most of the year – if that's been the agreement from day one then no problem. This may become more common as boards seek to diversify their director-base and become more global in their business footprint. In these cases, the company will have the requisite technology to set you up with proper IT connections so the board can see you in person (albeit on a screen or TV) for these meetings.

However, if your board is in the same town or country as you are, and the board has a written expectation or requirement that all meetings are to be attended in person or by other agreed means, then you have to make the commitment to attend these meetings.

If you are obliged to attend in person, and it's getting out of hand in terms of your inability to turn up meeting after meeting, then not only will your fellow directors, the executives and the secretariat notice but it also gives people a sense that your level of commitment to the organisation is questionable. Trust me, people see it. It might take a while for it to come up in conversation but at some point it will.

A few points to leave you with if joining the meeting offsite:

- **Phones:** Mute your phone for the meeting's duration, unless you and those in your surrounding environment can categorically stay very, very quiet and you can avoid moving your phone near your ear (an impossible task for anyone really). Any rustling of papers, chatting with your next door neighbour, child or spouse, birds chirping, trucks going past, the call of your airline or loud and ferocious typing at your PC are all examples of what's off-putting and annoying to those in the boardroom.

- **Don't type during the meeting** when you've joined by phone, as it's a dead giveaway that you are not 100% concentrating on the meeting. You'd be surprised how many people do this. Don't do it – it's a pain. And in a legal or regulatory proceeding, your computer or other electronic devices can be called for forensic examination. If it can be proven that you were doing things other than concentrating on your director role at the time then it can be problematic for you to explain this to your legal counsel, your board, chairman and any other party for whom this will cause difficulty or embarrassment.

- **Don't snack.** If joining by remote means, don't audibly snack, flush the toilet within earshot of the phone, do any other activities or make any noises that you wouldn't do in front of your fellow directors during a meeting in person. If you are having a break during the meeting, turn off the connection and re-start it once the meeting resumes. Don't leave it running – who knows what you could be sharing!

- **Don't text on your phone or tap your iPad.** We all know you absolutely must never text and drive, so don't do it during a board meeting either.

Here's a courtesy warning: the recommendation about not using electronic equipment when attending a meeting remotely also goes for anyone attending a board meeting in person – be it as a director or company secretary or legal counsel. You must be cognisant that any messages you send, any web-surfing you do, or any other electronically-linked activity undertaken during a board meeting is forensically traceable (regardless of the software program that will try and convince you otherwise) – and therefore if it's good fodder for the other side, it's up for grabs to put on the front page of the *Financial Review* if it hits the courts.

For all of the weeks and hours in a year that you have to read and send messages from any device, for the sake of your board schedule (as a relative percentage of the 8,760 hours there are in each year) please refrain from using them during a meeting. Everyone can see you are doing it – they are just too polite usually to let you know (or they feel bad because they are also doing it).

You may see the company secretary or equivalent on their iPhone or BlackBerry during the meeting – this is often because they are keeping tabs with those outside the boardroom on how the agenda is going and whether their item is late or early. Also, they may be conversing with those who arrange the catering and are waiting for an update on when the meeting break will come. It could also relate to technology or other matters critical to the meeting. Directors might also be running late and are conversing with the company secretary on when they are likely to arrive.

During the course of the meeting (especially for reasonably-sized companies), the minute-taker or secretary will usually be doing a multitude of things:

- Always taking the minutes
- Listening out for any disclosure requirements (if ASX-listed)
- Listening out for conflicts of interest, legal triggers or legal issues
- Keeping the chairman on track with the agenda
- Watching the time (always watching the time…)
- Sometimes recommending to the chairman that they cancel or re-schedule certain items
- Communicating with presenters outside regarding when to come into the boardroom
- Ensuring the room temperature is fine
- Checking on the catering
- Sending a search and rescue message to the board's techo guy to save them from an imminent disaster.

These roles encompass a multiplicity of tasks and responsibilities – it's an important attribute of the company secretary or minute-taker to be able to do many different things at once. So if you do see them on a device, they are most likely doing any one of the above things and are not giving the board carte blanche to be on emails or surfing the net.

10

ASKING QUESTIONS

THERE'S A LOT of information around about the right way to ask a question when you are in the boardroom. This is a skill which directors often need years of practice to be effective at. You want to phrase the question in such a way that it appears carefully considered and deliver it so people are convinced that you – as the director – genuinely believe that more information is required for the board to properly understand a certain matter or detail.

Some people say it's a craft that has to be honed through experience; you may have already developed this skill-set through your executive experience and so you may be much further along in this regard than others. If you are on your very first board and are totally unsure of how to best position or deliver your questions, my advice to you here is as follows:

- **Take from the best.** Take note of how other directors on the board pose their questions to management or visiting consultants (also watch the board and committee chairmen). From the person you believe is most effective or skilled at doing this, take note of what it is about how they phrase their questions that draws you in to think they are particularly effective in extracting the information out of the respondent. If you are comfortable in doing so, you might ask this director at the tea break or after the meeting to share their tips or insights into how they ask effective questions (especially if the industry is new to you).

- **Lead in with an apology or caveat.** Sometimes you may not ask a question in a particularly eloquent way, or you may come across as blunt, direct or clumsy – don't pressure yourself to be perfect in this regard when you are still very early into your tenure. You'll learn more each time you don't quite hit the mark. A briefly stated apology or caveat accompanying a difficult-to-construct question goes a long way, as it engenders empathy from the directors and management (because you are reflecting your courage to put yourself out there for the good of the board). Don't feel, however, that you must apologise or caveat every time – just do it when you are struggling to frame a difficult question as well as you'd like, or you just don't have sufficient experience to approach the question in what you think is the right way.

- **Think about how you would like the question to be pitched to you by a director if you were the respondent.** This may make it easier to re-work the content in your head. There is usually an etiquette followed at well-chaired meetings which all directors respect and uphold – this being that questions are generally raised 'through the chair'. You may see people raise their hands or send their eyes in the direction of the chairman during the conversation, indicating that they have a question. The chairman will generally give an acknowledging nod back to the director concerned, confirming that there is a question waiting. The chairman will endeavour to note the order in which questions are asked, to ensure fairness is applied with their colleagues. Those on the phone must both time and strongly vocalise the 'raising of their hands' usually once the presenter has stopped speaking or when the chairman calls for questions. Watch for how this works in practice and then follow the practice accordingly.

- **Quality – not quantity.** Considered, engaged, insightful, genuinely curious and respectfully-prodding questions are valued by both your fellow directors and management. You are on an important team being on this board and so you have to play your part. Some executives (not all – just some) can occasionally get irritated with directors asking them tonnes of questions, but it's less likely it will be their house or assets that will be on the line if the board gets it seriously wrong. If you know there's a big decision to be made at an upcoming meeting then try to do as much homework beforehand, be it with the CEO or other executives. Remember that while an expert's opinion or that of management can (and must) be duly considered by the board, it is each director's individual and independent assessment of the materials that matters when voting on the accompanying resolution. Also, recall how we discussed earlier the importance of taking in the culture of the board you are joining; of taking in the first meeting or two and sitting back and absorbing the behaviours, gestures and other rule-playing going on. This also applies to question-asking. Observe and take your cues from the best around the table.

As a director you are compelled by your legal duties to make sufficient independent enquiry in your own regard (and of course as a group) of company matters when contemplating whether to support a subject item or not.

There is definitely a level at which you need to ask questions of management outside of the boardroom. To determine what would qualify for out-of-boardroom questions, think about the materiality of the question relative to the item overall, where the board is at in its consideration of the entire matter and whether it's more for your information and learning, or a catch-up on history.

Is it something that will inform just you (and only you)? Or would the entire board benefit from being privy to it at a meeting? Is the question one which requires a detailed response that would be better comprehended by you in a written brief from management? Or putting on both your hindsight and directors' duties hats, is it a question that should be included in the board's deliberations on a particular matter and so needs to be shared for good decision-making (and potentially go into the minutes)?

What you never want to do (as obvious as it seems) is yell, swear, discredit or disrespect your fellow directors at the board table. If there's a board crisis afoot, then the dirty laundry needs to be aired outside of the boardroom with the director concerned – don't drag it through the boardroom in front of all and sundry. You also don't want to speak over your colleagues or management; nor do you heckle, humiliate, jibe, mock or insult your fellow directors or the executive. It's unprofessional and beneath your best self and it's embarrassing for you.

You may never agree with your fellow comrades on every decision – but that's not an open invitation to give your colleagues a witty smack around the ears for what you believe is their own stupidity or other unsavoury personality characteristic that doesn't sit well with you.

There's no issue with boards experiencing professional tension when making very significant or material decisions that will have profound impacts on the company and its future. From time to time, and when it's justifiable, that's a healthy commodity to have in the boardroom. As a group, the board needs to occasionally joust with itself to get to the best final decision or end point. The chairman plays an incredibly important role in these circumstances so take their leadership cue in managing any tension. Hopefully they are adept at exercising this skill with this particular director group.

What's decidedly not cool is any director asking questions with a bombastic, domineering or difficult tone, or asking questions to undermine the credibility of the respondent or others.

You are not compelled to ask questions at every meeting, on every paper. Some of the most effective directors ask very few questions, but when they do, it's because they genuinely feel devoid of a very important piece of information and without it they could not support a vote or resolution on the matter at hand.

> *"...I like asking questions, to keep learning;*
> *people with big egos may not want to look unsure."*
> *Heston Blumenthal*[26]

Asking the 'dumb' questions

Promise yourself something, for every single board that you ever go on to, always feel comfortable and entitled to ask what you might think are the dumb questions.

Recall the Enron case (if you're too young to remember it, Google it). There are certain cases that should stick in your corporate memory as a director regarding competencies, behaviours and decisions and Enron is one of those. Summarily, the case concerned the (now jailed for many years) CEO of a multi-billion dollar conglomerate being asked by a journalist whether the company had ever been profitable and how it made its money.

---

[26] www.brainyquote.com/quotes/quotes/h/hestonblum340419.html?src=t_asking_questions; accessed 28th March 2015

It was the quintessential case of no-one previously having asked this very question. How could that have ever been? Was it a cultural no-go or simply unfathomable for anyone to ask such 'basic' questions? Big lesson learned – huge.

The world needs more – not less – numbers of directors with the courage to ask what they or others might perceive as the 'dumb' questions.

Let's save the world from as many Enrons as we can.

There is a time and place to ask certain questions outside of the boardroom, particularly when you are in the very infancy of your appointment and are trying to piece together a very long sequence of events, for example. However, at some point you need to be able to stand back from what you've seen and learned and be confident to ask questions in the boardroom about matters that don't appear to add up, are not transparent enough for your purposes, or if you just can't connect A with B. If the chairman or CEO (or the person who wrote the paper) can't explain something to you in layman's terms, then what signal does that send to you? You would not be alone in your less than satisfactory understanding of this particular issue and under your director's duties of care and diligence in governing the company this comes profoundly into play.

Again it comes down to context, i.e. could it be something to be taken offline so that you can be walked through it in the required detail without holding up the board? Or could it be something that you just don't want to do offline and that you feel compelled to have answered at the table? There are distinct differences between these two scenarios and experience will help you through this muddle in your early tenure (seek the CEO's input and assistance if needed).

The golden rule is that you should not allow yourself to vote on a matter that you don't truly or sufficiently understand. It's better to ask the chairman to hold over the decision if possible, or you can consider abstaining and have the board's minutes reflect this. Don't put yourself into a pot of water and turn the gas up high to boil yourself alive, just because you didn't want to appear weak or intimidated in front of your fellow colleagues.

Another pragmatic option can sometimes be to vote on the content that you do support and understand and perhaps ask the board's permission to make the resolution conditional, i.e. upon you obtaining greater comfort in what's being proposed or getting more information later.

PART THREE

IN THE BOARDROOM AND BEYOND

"If gatekeepers fail in their role, it can have serious consequences for investors and our markets. This is why we hold gatekeepers – including directors – to account."

ASIC CHAIRMAN, GREG MEDCRAFT[27]

[27] www.companydirectors.com.au/Director-Resource-Centre/Publications/Company-Director-magazine/2014-back-editions/September/ASIC-Report; 1st September 2014 (Company Directors magazine); accessed 28th March 2015

11

BASIC DIRECTORS' DUTIES

"An investment in knowledge pays the best interest."

BENJAMIN FRANKLIN[28]

I HAVE TO preface this chapter with a reminder that you have to do your own research, before you accept a directorship, to make sure you are fully aware of what comprises your directors' duties. Please don't go away with the wrong impression, i.e. that what's in this chapter is all there is to know on this most important topic.

Directors' duties are some of the most critical components of our corporate governance system. In layman's terms, corporate governance can be explained as a system of policies, frameworks, processes and practices which, when united, ensures that companies don't become free-for-alls. Good corporate governance keeps Australia's companies and business landscapes robust, attractive for investors, and accountable to stakeholders and owners.

Given the importance of decisions taken by boards and the flow-on effects to the community, directors absolutely must be accountable

---

[28] www.brainyquote.com/quotes/authors/b/benjamin_franklin.html; accessed 28th March 2015

to each other, their employees, investors, shareholders, creditors and society itself which grants the company the licence to operate in the first place. It is the role of the governance community (including directors), regulators and the legal system to ensure that these duties are upheld for and on behalf of society, and it's your role and responsibility to ensure that you understand what your directors' duties are and to undertake your role as a board director with requisite respect of these rules, protocols and expectations.

I'm sure that if you've come this far in the book I'll have no argument from you on these points.

Like most crafts, there are insights and knowledge points that are critical for you to know. You don't have to be a walking *Corporations Act* or common law expert, nor do you need to be able to recall the vast volumes of case law that arise from this space. But what you do need to know in my opinion are the basics.

(Please note I don't account here for any industry-specific duties that may arise because, for example:

- You are a director on a superannuation board and because of this appointment you have extended duties under the *Superannuation Industry Supervision Act 1993* over and above those that apply under corporate law; or

- You are on a government board which is subject to specific Acts of Parliament; or

- You are on the board of an Aboriginal and Torres Strait Islander company which has some exemptions applying regarding directors' duties (refer *Corporations Act* s190B and see glossary at the back of the book).[29]

The duties discussed in this chapter are not exhaustive, are only

---

[29] www.austlii.edu.au/au/legis/cth/consol_act/ca2001172/s190b.html; accessed 28th March 2015

touched on at a high level, and are those duties which generally apply to most directors.

Before we get to directors duties, can we quickly consider your role as a fiduciary when appointed to a board. A fiduciary is an individual in whom another has placed the utmost trust and confidence to manage and protect property or money.[30] The essence of fiduciary duties as they apply to you as a director is that you have to put the interests of the company before any interests of your own.

To whom are duties owed?

The Australian Institute of Company Directors (AICD)[31] explains that a director's general statutory and fiduciary duty is owed to the organisation.

- **Directors do not owe duties to individual shareholders** (unless there is improper oppression of a minority shareholder).

- **Duties to non-shareholders (note that different companies have different attitudes to this):** There is no separate explicit legal duty under the *Corporations Act* owed by companies and directors to society as a whole; however the duty to act in the interests of the organisation cannot be done in isolation to the exclusion of other stakeholders.

- **Duty to the company group:** Each company in a group is a separate legal entity, with directors owing duties to the company to which they are appointed. There are conditional provisions which can be put in place through a subsidiary's constitution to allow that company to act in the best interests of the parent.

- **Duties to creditors:** Directors do not owe a separate legal duty to creditors – protection for creditors is through the insolvent

---

30 http://legal-dictionary.thefreedictionary.com/fiduciary; accessed 23rd November 2014
31 www.companydirectors.com.au/Courses/Courses-for-the-Director/Company-Directors-Course, accessed 22 February 2015

trading provisions of the *Corporations Act*. However the Bell Group case stated the need to take the interests of creditors into account to discharge your duty to act in the best interests of the company and for a proper purpose.

Corporations Act

The *Corporations Act* holds the rules which apply to companies in Australia. You can find the *Act* online or in printed version – the online version is found at www.austlii.edu.au.[32]

Users of the *Act* are extensive: directors, regulators, courts, lawyers, company secretaries, governance advisers, academics and students.

Because of the onus on you to undertake your own education on directors' duties, and because this book is merely meant to be a conversation starter on what to look for as a director, I am only going to touch on the *Corporations Act* provisions (and lightly at that) – just to whet your appetite to go and search out more information, or to enrol in an appropriate training course.

Directors' duties

Directors' duties are governed by the company's constitution, the *Corporations Act 2001* and the common law (judge-made law, creating precedents to be followed in later cases).

The section of common law for directors' duties is massive and has been progressively built up over decades from judges applying legislated law (and sometimes equity) to real-world situations. As you progress in your reading and education, you'll find a strong overlap in some common law and legislated directors' duties.

Proper training will provide you with a requisite insight into all directors' duties covered in the *Act*, but in particular those in **Division 1**:

---

[32] www.austlii.edu.au/cgi-bin/sinodisp/au/legis/cth/consol_act/ca2001172/index.html#s1.5.1; accessed 28th March 2015

- Care and diligence (s180)
- Good faith (s181)
- Use of position (s182)
- Use of information (s183)
- Good faith, use of position and use of information – criminal offences (s184)
- Reliance on information or advice provided by others (s189)
- Responsibility for actions of delegate (s190).

Division 2 duties cover the disclosure of and voting on matters involving material personal interests:

- Material personal interest – directors' duty to disclose (s191)
- Standing notice about an interest (s192)
- Interaction of ss191 and 192 with other laws (s193)
- Voting and completion of transactions – directors of proprietary companies (replaceable rule) (s194)
- Restrictions on voting for directors of public companies (s195).

One incredibly important section (s588G) covers a director's duty to prevent insolvent trading by the company. This is a highly complex subject but to summarise:

- A person commits an offence if a company incurs a debt at a particular time; and
- At that time, a person is a director of the company; and
- The company is insolvent at that time (or becomes insolvent by incurring that debt); and
- There are reasonable grounds for a person to suspect at the time that the company was insolvent (or would become insolvent as a result of incurring that debt or other debts).

If dishonesty is involved it then becomes a criminal offence. There is a large body of case law that has been created through testing this section of the *Act*, and it's an incredibly important piece of legislation to protect the community, the company's shareholders and creditors. It places a considerable and rightful onus on the directors of a company to ensure that the company remains solvent when conducting its business. It also provides directors with a significant impetus to call in expert assistance to assist the board to understand whether the company is insolvent or potentially insolvent (if you ever reach that point), and what steps could be taken to mitigate or address current circumstances.

You will also learn through an appropriate financials course that these days it's more the cash flow test used to measure the extent of solvency (or otherwise) of a company, rather than the net balance sheet position.

As stated earlier in the pre-appointment section of the book, be very astute in your dealings as a director in monitoring whether the company is solvent, and take guidance or advice (if you don't know otherwise) as to what the potential signs of insolvency are.

> **TIP:** *The Company Directors course and other financial courses available through the AICD, and university courses on applied corporate governance provide an excellent outline of this for directors but so too does the internet through easy-to-understand cases and examples.*

Sections of interest

Here are some sections of the *Act* which it's good to be familiar with (if they happen to be applicable to your situation), outside of the directors' duties:

Part 1.2A	Disclosing Entities (if your company is ASX-listed)
Part 2B.1	Covers the basic features of a company (legal capacity and powers, executing documents, etc.)

Part 2B.4	Replaceable rules and constitution
s187	Directors of wholly-owned subsidiaries
s197	Directors liable for debts and other obligations incurred by corporation as trustee
198A	Powers of directors (replaceable rule – see section 135)
198B	Negotiable instruments (replaceable rule – see section 135)
198C	Managing director (replaceable rule – see section 135)
198D	Delegation
198E	Single director/shareholder proprietary companies
198F	Right of access to company books
Chapter 2G	Meetings (for directors and members)
Part 2G.3	Minutes
Chapter 6CA	Continuous disclosure (mainly for listed entities)

The residual sections of the *Act* not noted above (and there are hundreds of them!) are generally more of interest to those persons in the company who are charged with its legal and compliance administration.

The *Act* is extensive and can be complicated, so that's why I encourage you take an instructed or guided course through an education-provider so that you can get to know the basic components.

Further reading on directors' duties

Don't be overwhelmed by the directors' duties and the provisions that apply to being a director – just be proactive, educated and informed. Over time, their application to your director work will become more seamless. Seek help. Get yourself educated. Ask questions. Research. It's all part of the deal of going onto a board and representing all the various interests that are at stake.

Some excellent guides on the internet include:

- *A Guide to Directors Duties and Responsibilities for Non-Listed Public and Proprietary Companies in Australia*[33] from PWC – this guide provides not only a list of the most relevant directors' duties but also common law provisions and examples of breaches (so you can see where and how other directors have got themselves into hot water). It's one of the best, easiest-to-understand guides that I've seen on directors' duties (it's not onerous in size or complexity). The discussion of common law duties in particular is recommended reading.
- Information on the ASIC website: www.asic.gov.au
- FindLaw Australia articles
- Information on the Company Directors website: www.companydirectors.com.au
- Other compilations by private organisations that summarise directors' duties and when these change
- You can also look up most law firms' websites (particularly the bigger ones that specialise in corporate law, e.g. King Wood Mallesons), to get a feeling for what comprises directors' duties and how these are applied in reality. You'll be totally spoilt for choice, so take your pick on what works for you as you start on your first board.

Also, if you sign up as a recipient of the *Company Director* magazine issued monthly by the AICD, you can use its articles to progressively build up your knowledge and stay in touch with changes to directors' duties during your board career.

Loads of directors don't educate themselves on these duties and often have very little cognisance of the potential for law-suits or what

---

[33] http://etraining.communitydoor.org.au/pluginfile.php/608/course/section/95/GuideDirectors_Apr08.pdf

constitutes inappropriate behaviour in the eyes of the law or our statutory authorities. More important than avoiding law suits, being strongly cognisant of directors' duties will grow your confidence and build your knowledge such that you will know when something going on is not quite right (it's all about the light going on) – trust me, it will help you to sleep easier at night.

12

ACTIVITIES BEYOND THE BOARDROOM

IN THIS CHAPTER we will cover off the following few topics that might seem a bit flung together but they are actually singularly important to note and consider:

- Board offsites
- Board dinners
- Industry events
- Interviews and communications
- Discussing board business
- Dropping by the office.

Board offsites

It is now a very common practice for boards to hold offsites or board strategy day/s at least once per year, or once every two years.

Notwithstanding the growth in this practice, whether your board will do these will depend on the type and size of company you are joining and whether they think it is warranted, or if the board has an appetite for it (in terms of people's time, the cost, the arrangements, pre-work to be done, how much it contributes to strategy, etc.).

If the company is even a decent-sized enterprise you should expect to see a board offsite or strategy day in the board calendar at least once a year. If there's absolutely no sign of one in the calendar, then ask your chairman why. The reason why board offsites are important is that they are offline (out of the office) opportunities for the entire board, the CEO and the executives to get away from the business of running the company or corporate group, to discuss, debate, test and fine-turn the company's future strategies (or amendments to) with clear and concentrated heads.

These are important discussions because the events are not minuted (well none I've ever been to have been) and so directors have the opportunity to speak freely and openly on how they really feel about certain matters. They also provide a very important opportunity for the board and the executives to have a more relaxed, fluid and candid dialogue across a whole range of topics that may not always be freely discussed at the board table by either party.

Offsites, planning days or strategy retreats all try to achieve essentially the same thing – to get clarity, agreement and fresh commitment from both the board and the executives on how to drive the company forward in an aligned manner.

If your company is in disarray because of some particular issue or event, it could be that the offsite is more of a crisis forum and deliberation on which way is forward from here, providing an opportunity to explore options such as mitigants, further risks, opportunities, etc. Otherwise, you may find your group addressed by pre-selected external parties who have been brought in to share their experience on getting through a crisis and what they would do again both the same and differently.

For the newbie director, these are immensely educational opportunities as you are in a safe environment to openly share your feedback and to hear from others regarding what they see happening in the company. You can also be on the receiving end of some significant creativity and energy.

The session could include presentations from other consultants, the CEO and the executives. Sometimes the board will assign directors particular topics to steer or introduce at the offsite (so perhaps requiring some pre-work on your behalf in conjunction with other executives or directors).

> **TIP:** *Any which way your offsite goes, it is an absolute imperative that you attend. As a director it shows distinct commitment to the company, and to the executives it confirms your professional engagement with the company and the road ahead.*

An offsite gives you such an invaluable opportunity to mingle with and get to know the executives and your fellow directors which can provide you with so much more confidence and comfort when you're back inside the boardroom. Knowing just a few small things about your directors as fellow human beings will also make a world of difference to your first few years of tenure.

The sessions can confirm or illuminate why the executives are wanting to take the company forward in a certain direction. The opportunity for new directors to be in among this discussion, debate and deliberation is golden, even if it does take a couple of days out of your business week.

Things that are decided at the offsite can also set the scene for the work program in the coming year or years. So if you've missed out on the sessions which will be the first building blocks of the new strategy or business plan, then you could be behind the eight ball once you return to the boardroom.

Not only that, if you don't attend your absence will require another member of the board or the CEO to take you through outcomes and next steps decided at the offsite. If it is the case that you have a qualifying reason for not attending, then ensure you notify the chairman and CEO well ahead of time and arrange for a suitable de-brief after the offsite has been held.

Board dinners

Which brings us to our next topic – somewhat related to offsites – board dinners. Socialising with your fellow directors is incredibly important and I strongly encourage you to accept as many invitations as your diary allows – it can be a pre-board meeting dinner with all directors (so held the night before the meeting starts), or it can be held at other times during the year.

These are opportunities to significantly build upon new and longer-standing relationships at the board. They provide a relaxed, non-minuted environment for directors to put things on the table which might concern them or they might be enthusiastic about, for example there may be new opportunities on the horizon or a new direction in the company's strategy.

Board dinners provide the chairman with great insights into how their board is thinking about certain topics and therefore can make the chairing of the next or future meetings much smoother or more efficient. They also allow rapport to build between newer directors and those who have been appointed for a longer period of time and this brings them closer in their understanding of each other's position on certain topics and/or provides an insight into a person's background and influences.

These occasions really can be tremendously valuable to all members of the board. They are opportunities for directors and the chairman to openly and robustly discuss very important matters regarding the company and thus provide a unique perspective for the team to hear about how others are feeling on certain matters such as the age-old question "what keeps you awake at night?"

Your attendance at these events again is a signal of your commitment and collegiality and quite frankly it is just a grown-up expectation that directors have of each other. As with offsites, these social events offer an opportunity to get to know your colleagues outside of the boardroom and this is priceless. You are encouraged to attend these events even if you are terrified of professional social interactions generally, or just despise spending your valuable free time with people you probably wouldn't choose to be friends with. Well that's a bit of tough luck because you are all in this game together and so this expectation comes with the territory.

If you are introverted or shy when you first meet and socialise with people, don't let that get in the way of making this happen. You must grit your teeth and get through it. Just be yourself, you will congratulate yourself and feel better for going once it's done. Unless your day job is emergency medicine or the emergency services, for example, and you genuinely need to be excused from an event, excuses such as I'm tired, or I have to work, won't cut it with your colleagues. If one's in, you are all in.

Industry and company events

Away from the boardroom, but still part of your role as director, may be attendance at industry and company events. Now this one will be entirely dependent on the type of company you join and the board's activities generally in and around company or industry events. I know that I caveat a lot, but each board, company and industry can be very different on this topic.

So what you need to know when such invitations or events come your way is whether it's compulsory to attend, where they are being held and what is your role there as a director.

For example, if you are on the board of a theatre company, art gallery, orchestra, music festival or a company that hosts events for the public, then you will be expected to patronise these – at least once for each event or performance, play or exhibition. You will be expected to mingle with other directors or executives, meet some of your company's donors (if applicable) to discuss their interest in, or connection to, the company, the public or cast.

Your attendance depends to some extent on the type and size of company, where the events are located and what role the directors traditionally play. For example, if the National Australia Bank opens a new branch somewhere in Australia and there's an opening ceremony held by the branch manager to celebrate this, then obviously no-one from the board is either going to be invited or will be expected to show up (and neither should they be expected to). However, if you are on the board of the Australian Ballet and have never, ever seen a performance, or you have joined the soccer club's board and have never attended a game, then there's something wrong with your connection to and interest in the company.

If your (grass roots) company is fundraising for a national, state or local cause then why wouldn't you be personally supportive of this activity? This might involve anything from you having to turn up to the sausage sizzle at an ungodly hour on a cold and wet Sunday morning at Bunnings, to delivering a cheque to the CEO from a donor or depositing some of your own money into the fundraising account (if that's an expectation of the directors on your board).

When there is an expectation for directors to be present at the company's events, your participation will be incredibly important and give a clear indication of your genuine interest in the company and its causes.

Everything has a context, so get the lay of land in terms of whether there are expectations on directors to attend and support events. It could be that management simply wants to run a great event, e.g. a product launch or opening of a new outlet, without the presence of directors. They may actually not want the directors anywhere near it!

So take some guidance from your CEO or chairman as to expectations – especially in your first year.

Interviews and communications

At some point you may find yourself on the board of a company that's particularly interesting to those on the outside world, such as journalists, social commentators, talk show hosts, politicians and social media bloggers or opinion influencers.

Therefore you may be called upon with or without notice to make off-the-cuff or spontaneous comments, provide a considered opinion or to be interviewed about your life and achievements (including how you came to be on this board).

> **CAUTION:** *You need to be absolutely 100% clear on what the company's policies are regarding who is authorised to make public comment about the company. This includes what media are acceptable to the company (social media, print or TV), and whether, for example, the copy or result of the encounter has to be proofed and passed by the external affairs or investor relations person before it's released.*

This can be an absolute mine-field and terribly risky, so be incredibly careful, well prepared or well advised. Ask yourself or the person seeking the information why they are coming to you for insights and not the communications and external affairs departments, or the office of the CEO. If you are on the board of a very small company with no external affairs staff (or anyone in the company or on the board with this experience) then you should run the interview or request for a quote through the chairman or the CEO before making public comment specifically about the company.

Companies usually have very clear and precise guidelines around who is authorised to speak publicly on company matters – these are usually for the chairman, CEO and/or the head of external affairs.

If ever in doubt, the good ol' response of 'no comment' can be your holding point pending getting further advice.

Think before you share

Also, once you are a director, I'd advise you to be hyper aware of engaging in social media on topics that could land you in hot water.

How many times do we read in the press about some presumably well-meaning director who has expressed their personal views on topics which have the capacity to raise the significant scorn of the Australian public – and it's gone exactly that way. People do sometimes lose sight of what they think is private and what is public (as well as what is authorised comment about a company and what is not).

Don't fool yourself into thinking that anything you put in an email, SMS, USB, Facebook entry, Twitter feed, Instagram, Pinterest, You Tube, LinkedIn, Tumbler or other like medium can't or isn't going to be re-tweeted, shared or publicly held against you for future debate, justification or ridicule. Depending on the content of what you say or share, you could put not only your own personal and public reputation on the line but you could also do irreparable damage to the board and a company you respect.

If you are truly bothered by something you've seen online or in social media and you strongly believe the company should be publicly responding, either walk away, ignore it or take advice from your internal advisers at the company, including the CEO.

Once your response or comments are out there, they are forensically retrievable and remain in existence forever – regardless of you removing your profile, your post or comment. If it's been sent somewhere in an electronic medium then it's out there – FOREVER – and you can never take it back.

Discussing board business outside the boardroom

OK, so you might think this section is a bit obvious, as who would even consider discussing their boardroom activities with people outside?

You'll be under a confidentiality agreement (which is a contract), probably a separate director's contract and may be subject to other commentary restrictions (not the least being the common law, ASX listing rules and your fiduciary duties). The duties exist simultaneously and in parallel:

> "...even in circumstances where the contract expressly provides for obligations to protect confidential information, an equitable duty of confidence can co-exist with the contractual duty".[34]

It's not only facts and information that are captured by insider trading and other laws but also that are discussed around the board table.[35]

---

[34] www.companydirectors.com.au/Director-Resource-Centre/Publications/Company-Director-magazine/ 2013-back-editions/May/Opinion-The-importance-of-keeping-secrets; accessed 19th October 2014

[35] www.lw.com/upload/pubContent/_pdf/pub2916_1.pdf; accessed 19th October 2014

Here are some tips for how you can manage information that has come into your possession by means of your membership on this board.

Don't share the information with your partner, children, friends, neighbours, the local 7-Eleven or anyone else, regardless of whether you know or believe that they will never act on the information or use it for their own (or your) benefit – or procure others to use the information.

> **WARNING:** *Never share confidential boardroom or confidential company information with anyone outside of the board sphere unless you have prior written consent from the company.*

However harmless it might seem at the time, it can come home to bite you in a very big, public and ugly way. Quite simply, it's the wrong thing to do (equitably and on a fiduciary basis) and it can be a breach of your contract with the company.

If you are appointed to a board as a result of your nominator's shareholding in the company, then you need to take particular guidance from the company secretary, head of governance, risk or the legal counsel on what (if any) information can be shared back with your appointing organisation (on what basis or in what circumstances). Be very sure and clear on these parameters before sharing anything with your shareholder or sponsoring colleagues.

The confidentiality provisions that you are subject to across all facets of the law are incredibly important safeguards for the interests of the company's shareholders and support the country's laws in commerce. Penalties can apply if you breach your confidentiality provisions, be they pecuniary (so fines) but also non-pecuniary (ASIC action, reputational damage, etc). And that's before the company sues you.

'Discussing' means sharing information verbally one-on-one, talking over the phone (either in private or publicly), chatting at your Sunday barbeque or being a bit too liberal with an information exchange, e.g. when at the hairdressers or on the train. It can also mean sending, sharing or disseminating information by any electronic or paper means.

If a member of the public recognises you (in public) as being a director on a company's board and they try to engage you in a conversation about a certain matter, don't go anywhere near contentious issues or those which are highly confidential or discussed in the boardroom. If you are in a very public area, never discuss anything unless it's publicly known and released. Always thank the person for their interest in the company and try and engage them in a positive conversation (if that's what's required to keep some order and discretion in the conversation). If they totally despise the company and anyone or thing to do with it, thank them for the feedback and refer them through to the company's complaints line or contacts page on the website (unless the circumstances warrant you taking down their details to pass onto the right person at the company who can help them). If they already love the company then always thank them for their patronage or membership and genuinely encourage them to continue their connection with the company.

Dropping by the office

Short and sharp here: generally directors are not seen liberally and frequently wandering the offices of their board's company (in management's trenches) unless they are attending a meeting there, or it's a pre-announced site visit, or they are meeting with the CEO or the executives to discuss a paper or particular matter of business.

It might be that this is where the chairman keeps their office and you are meeting with them to have your individual director's performance review, or you are discussing your potential appointment as a member to, or chairman of, one of the board's committees. You might also visit to return papers to the company secretary for disposal or to sign documents.

It is neither an expected nor common sight (in my experience) to see non-executive directors trawling the hallways and corridors of the premises out of which the company operates. There is a fine though distinct line that the board has to walk in not wandering over into the territory of management and in over-stepping its role in daily business life.

So unless you need to be on the premises for a particular reason, you probably shouldn't be hanging about the office too much at all. You may be given the use of a desk or office if you are in town and are between appointments, or you need to drop off your suitcase for safe keeping – absolutely no problem. But don't stalk the poor people who are doing the hard yards in the office. Give them respectful space to do their jobs without being a pesky director looking over their shoulder.

"The way a team plays as a whole determines its success. You may have the greatest bunch of individual stars in the world, but if they don't play together, the club won't be worth a dime" Babe Ruth [36]

---

[36] www.brainyquote.com/quotes/quotes/b/baberuth125974.html; accessed 28th March 2015

13

THE KEY RELATIONSHIPS

WHO, YOU MIGHT ask, are the people that I really need to get to know in the company and why?

You might think this is an obvious subject and for some people with their backgrounds it will be. However, if you are brand new to this game and haven't actually had a lot to do with boards in your day job (or indeed very large companies that are multi-layered in their organisational design), then it's helpful to have an insight into some key corporate roles that have a lot to do with the board.

I'm using my own experience and reflections in this section but you can most certainly build on this through courses undertaken with the AICD or other education-providers.

You need to remember that there are as many types and combinations of roles in companies as there are stars in the sky (same as for directors and boards). So often there will be nuances with what these roles do, on a day-to-day basis. I'll stick to generalisations to give you a sufficient head-start for when you commence your first board tenure.

Chairman

Let's start with the boss of the board – the chairman. Now this can be a contentious thing to say but it's the truth. This has been my experience for every board that I've worked with and I have seen or read little to dispel it. Nothing will happen at your board unless the chairman wants it to, or concedes to it happening. That is, unless you've been appointed to a board with a totally limp-fish for a chairman and the rest of the board (or parts thereof) are really running the show. If that is not the case, then this role is almost 100% likely to be the most influential (on balance) in your boardroom.

You may have heard the saying that the chairman is the first amongst equals – Wikipedia says it comes from the Latin phrase *Primus inter pares* and is:

> "…*typically used as an honorary title for those who are formally equal to other members of their group but are accorded unofficial respect, traditionally owing to their seniority in office*".[37]

The chairman is the senior leader of the board and has numerous tasks to complete over and above those of the general director. Theirs is a high-profile role with more internal and external interfaces. They are sometimes afforded additional delegations of authority to do certain things outside of board meetings, e.g. to sign documents to support the expeditious execution of company matters. It may also be that some decisions (depending on the company's circumstances) need to be made between board meetings and the directors have concurred (through a prior agreed delegation) that they have total comfort and confidence in the chairman undertaking these tasks or approvals on their behalf. These are sometimes legal or governance-based authorities.

---

[37] http://en.wikipedia.org/wiki/Primus_inter_pares; accessed 2nd November 2014

The combination of the chairman's skills, commercial and board experience, education and confidence will be among some of the critical factors in determining how well the board will be governed. Their qualities, capabilities and experience can make or break your own experience on a board.

A poor experience will come from a chairman who is any one or a combination of difficult, inexperienced, bombastic, biased, timid, intimidating, intimidated or uncommitted.

Getting the chairman's appointment wrong is likely to be a fundamental problem for the board and can undermine the board's immediate and long-term stability, effectiveness, collegiality and governance strength.

You will not find a definition of a chairman in the *Corporations Act*.[38] Instead, a highly topical and well-discussed role in governance circles, its function has been developed over decades of board practices, agreed procedures and customs and common law findings.[39]

On occasion, the law (and in turn, Australia's governance circles) turns its mind to the question of whether there are additional responsibilities which attach to being the chairman[40] – one of the more closely explored cases was that made against the One.Tel chairman (Greaves).

This case explored whether the chairman had additional, special responsibilities relative to other directors. Online literature neither supports nor agrees with some of the points made by the Justices, who considered that the chairman does indeed have such responsibilities. The Australian Institute of Company Directors (AICD) does not

---

[38] www.companydirectors.com.au/Director-Resource-Centre/Director-QA/Roles-Duties-and-Responsibilities/Role-of-the-Chairman; accessed 2nd February 2015

[39] www.companydirectors.com.au/Director-Resource-Centre/Director-QA/Roles-duties-and-responsibilities/Role-of-the-Chairman; accessed 21 October 2014

[40] www.allens.com.au/pubs/pdf/ldr/focnapr03.pdf; accessed 21st October 2014

support the notion that the chairman's role comes with heightened or extended responsibilities. As held in their paper released post One.Tel, the AICD stated that:

> *"The legal duties and responsibilities of the chairman match those of other board members, as board decisions are the collective responsibility of the board regardless of the individual skills, backgrounds or qualifications of each member".*[41]

In any case, the chairman's role is considerably more extensive than that of the normal director so if you ever aspire to such a post, you would need to first appreciate the extra components that go with this appointment. Chairmen don't get paid more than you do (if you get paid) for simply sitting at the head of the table and deciding when you all break for morning tea!

Blended CEO/chairman

Your chairman will be termed as one who is either fully independent of the company and its shareholders, and who meets an agreed test of independence (be it a test termed by the company or that adopted by the ASX), or they will be an executive chairman which means they will hold the roles of CEO and chairman simultaneously.

The latter is someone who is involved in the day-to-day management of the company but is also the leader of the board. This model of blending the CEO and chairman's roles can be found across a range of companies including very small ones, often in family corporations, but also in some very large organisations – including ASX-listed entities such as Harvey Norman and News Corp. At Harvey Norman, not only is Gerry Harvey a major shareholder and executive chairman, but he is also the husband of the CEO – Katie Page.

---

[41] www.companydirectors.com.au/~/media/Resources/Director%20Resource%20Centre/
Policy%20on%20director%20issues/2006/200601%20Greaves%20case%20%20
responsibilities%20%20liabilities%20of%20chairman.ashx; accessed 21st October 2014

Other blended CEO/chairman roles may include chairmen who are appointed by a party designated by the constitution and so are not considered one hundred per cent independent by ordinary tests, but they also do not work in the business and so are not 'executive' chairmen either.

The current argument goes that if your chairman is fully independent of all forms of associations with the company then they will be able to operate and conduct themselves totally free of interference from any other party, and will therefore be able to more successfully direct the board in its role to govern over the company. In my experience with boards (and that of plenty of other governance professionals and directors I know), the question of independence – be it about the chairman or the directors – comes down to this: the absolute ability of a person to stand back and clinically consider and make decisions based on what is truly the best outcome for the organisation, its shareholders and stakeholders. This is a capability devoid of overt external or internal influence – it's a true independence of the mind.

A genuine commitment to the company and a forward-looking strategic outlook, coupled with an unrestrained ability to question and probe what's being put in front of them will always win out over an academically-constructed definition, based on which side of a fence you sit on.

Taking a cookie-cutter approach to mandating board compositions is, in my mind, fraught with danger and lacks true insight and experience into understanding what actually makes a great board.

Chairman's duties

As stated earlier, the chairman's role is much more extensive than yours will be, if you are a director only. If you are terribly fortunate enough to be paid for your tenure (don't worry if it's not part of the deal for your first appointment) you should expect a discernible difference between the chair's remuneration and yours. This is to compensate them for the relatively greater amount of time and commitment that goes with the chairman's role, including the more extensive out-of-boardroom work that is done with the CEO, connecting with the market and investors, philanthropists, stakeholders, shareholders, and governments and the annual and ongoing review of the board's composition and performance.

Effectively chairing board meetings is one of the most essential skills of the chairman. The role also ensures (or should) that there are appropriate succession plans in place for the CEO and directors, as well as overseeing the most critical or significant governance matters undertaken by the board.

The arrangement of the board's calendar will usually start with the availability of your chairman (as might many other governance and operational practices). Chairmen will usually also want to stamp their mark on board procedures and board operational matters (those which are allowed under law or common practice to be alternated according to individual preferences).

The chairman is likely to have a very great influence on your ongoing tenure. If the chairman does not believe you are doing your share of the heavy lifting at the board, or that you are bringing the requisite or expected capabilities or qualities to the table, then they may call you in for a discussion or evaluation of the longer-term role you will play with the company.

The chairman is to be utilised to vet any serious concerns you have about any part of the board's operations or that of the company. They may also be used to raise new ideas with. Your relationship should be cordial, respectful and open and never clingy, argumentative or dismissive.

At the commencement of your due diligence to join the board, and when you first meet with the chairman, assure yourself that this will be a person you can work alongside and support in their leadership of the board. It is a critical relationship that you will have during your tenure and it is to be progressively built upon, respected and valued, though never over-used or abused to either person's benefit or disadvantage.

Where do the shareholders figure in the 'boss of the company' stakes?

If the chairman is the boss of the board (as discussed earlier), they are not the technical boss of the company – that title goes to the shareholders.

Each company's constitution (approved by the shareholders) states how the board is to be appointed and by whom. This may also include selection of the chairman. The board then chooses the CEO, and the CEO appoints everyone else. So it all starts and ends with the shareholders.

Now this is not to over-simplify or ignore the issues which can arise in the law regarding what can and can't be done by the shareholders and the board – that can get crazy-complicated. But what I'm saying is that without the shareholders, there is no company and therefore no board. So the shareholders are the cement footing of the company from which the walls, ceiling and the roof of the house are built.

The chief executive officer

The CEO is the boss of the operating company and is appointed and removed by the board – therefore the CEO could have between three and 16 bosses! And that's before their employees, shareholders, regulators, the legal system and stakeholders all pitch in with their say. It's a very tough but special gig.

The CEO is someone you should see at every board meeting and often at every board committee meeting. They'll obviously also attend the annual general meeting (AGM) and board offsites (if you have them). They will front the company's major external events and can also be the media, analyst and investor contact point (though not always exclusively).

Sometimes the CEO is also an executive director appointed to the board – thus becoming what's known as a managing director. This can be a tricky role as it straddles the day-to-day CEO components, and then converts to a directorship when it comes time to sit at the board table.

Any which way it goes, the CEO will play a key role when considering your relationship with the company. Your relationship with the CEO is a little akin to the one you will have with the chairman; however, as a regular director on the board, you do not have a hotline straight through to the CEO on any and every matter that takes your fancy. They are not your friend; they are not someone for you to boss around or fetch you endless reams of information. This person is the conduit between the board and the business, and your relationship should ideally be (as with the chairman) respectful, give-and-take, open though direct and conducted in the best interests of the company. There needs to be some space between the roles. It's a professional relationship.

You should not expect the CEO to provide you with a permanent office in the company's building, or extensive free secretarial assistance, just because you are a director (unless it's offered to you as part of your appointment, for whatever lucky or bizarre reason).

To succeed according to expectations, the CEO must have the unanimous support and confidence of the board. If the board feels as though the CEO is not cutting it, performance-wise, the board should be meeting 'in camera' or without the presence of management to discuss privately any lingering or building concerns on this point. If performance becomes an issue, it's also likely that an (engaged) chairman has already started to have private conversations with the CEO to work out what's going on and whether it can be rectified. Sometimes the issues are simply insurmountable and the board will be asked to review the ongoing tenure of the incumbent.

The CEO's capabilities, experience, skills, education, resources, attitude and extent of authority held to run the company will be some of the most critical factors which determine whether the company will deliver on the approved strategy and business plan.

They certainly do not do it all by themselves – their role is made up of all of the individual parts of the company they oversee. But it starts and ends with them.

It's not only their technical or commercial qualities, experience and capabilities as a CEO that count it's their ability to liaise appropriately but skilfully with stakeholders external to the company, their ability to build and uphold a strong internal culture, to liaise with and manage investors, media and regulators.

Regardless of the company's size, these are big, big roles that any director who's ever been a CEO (or worked closely with one) will know. You will perhaps then be more sensitive or intuitive when reviewing their performance.

However, that's not to say you should go soft on them just because it's such a big job. The board needs to balance its empathies when warranted, supporting the CEO through difficult times; but then always holding them to account for what it is they are there for – to deliver on performance and strategy.

During your induction or due diligence you can enquire with the CEO what their preferences are regarding inter-board meeting contact.

Seek to establish an open, supportive though independent and cordial relationship with your CEO – respect their boundaries and work out (over time) what the best approach is to working alongside them. It's also a great idea to spend time with the CEO at board offsites and during board meeting breaks, as it allows you each to get to know one another better as individuals outside of a minuted environment.

Finally, the directors need to be able to challenge the CEO at the board table when the occasion calls for it and it will be a test of the collective relationships as to how this principle holds up in the good times and bad.

Company secretary

Remember…this entire book is coming to you from a seasoned governance practitioner. A reminder of why that perspective is really valuable and why you might want to take this opinion on board is that company secretaries and governance practitioners see the very best and worst of directors – in their contributions and behaviours. They are therefore sometimes the best people to take insights from (especially if you are joining your first board and you have a great company secretary or secretariat in place).

Professional company secretaries and practitioners are often (but not always) legally qualified, or have backgrounds in finance, management, compliance and risk. In very large companies they may occupy senior and influential positions and will have the ear of the chairman, CEO and entire executive. They are generally well connected externally and often are the company's connection with regulators and sometimes shareholders. Outside of the basics that everyone does, the role can be a chocolate box of duties and responsibilities – it's entirely bespoke to the company concerned.

Depending on the company's size, complexity, resources and structural preferences, the role can be singular (so someone's full-time day job) or it can be rolled into another senior role in the finance, legal or compliance area.

Company secretaries and governance practitioners develop a deep knowledge of all matters covered in this book, as well as a company's history, the key players, and how culture operates. They may also attend the executive meetings which further broadens their understanding of the company's key strategies and material matters. Their opinions are valued and sought after because they have perspective. They would be up there with the most qualified in the company to speak to the company's and board's culture.

The company secretary is going to be with you throughout your journey with this board and so they are an incredibly knowledgeable and resourceful contact.

The breadth of the role of a company secretary is never less than extensive – especially if it's a full-time role. Those who do it in parallel with another day-job are to be commended for their ability to combine the two roles – it's not easy given the variety of work involved (but also the responsibilities).

Just for one physical board meeting alone (leading into and at the meeting) their range of activities might include:

- Taking care of director and presenter invitations, transport, hotels
- Arranging or overseeing the catering order (ensuring no-one collapses from a fatal food allergy)
- Being mindful of the meeting room temperature (meetings don't work when it's freezing cold – no one concentrates)
- Ensuring professional quality board packs are delivered to all directors at the agreed time
- Taking quality minutes
- Getting agendas pre-approved
- Getting the minutes signed post-meeting

- Managing tabled papers
- Ensuring there is a quorum at the meeting at all times
- Directing the chairman on a multitude of issues during the meeting (timings, agenda re-ordering)
- Keeping an eye on the legal issues, disclosure points or conflicts of interest
- Disposal of any board papers post-meeting (if that's the practice)
- File the approved and signed minutes in the minute book
- Inform later anyone not present if their papers were approved at the meeting
- In their spare time, ensure that the technology works for each and every presenter or director joining the meeting by means other than in person!

And that list doesn't include regulatory or annual work program items.

It's a huge role and one that needs exceptional co-ordination, planning, forward-thinking, mitigation strategies, the ability to clearly and confidently direct and engage support staff and importantly the ability to guide, direct and support the chairman, CEO and the board.

Things you should know about the company secretary:

- The company secretary is appointed and removed by the board; they have a direct line of accountability to the board, as well as an independent referral line to the chairman should they see or suspect any funny business going on in the trenches. The *Corporations Act 2001* deals with their legal appointment and responsibilities.
- They and the governance practitioner or general manager equivalent are often trusted advisers to the chairman, CEO, board and executives on matters such as best-practice corporate governance, board operations, shifts in company culture and

regulatory matters.

- They are diplomats, observers, tacticians, negotiators, enforcers; they are usually highly pedantic but also resilient; they may be harmonisers and idealists. If it's their full-time gig, I can guarantee you that they will be among the hardest working people in your company.

- You should make it your business to get to know the company secretary and, depending on the size of the company, their personal assistant (PA) and others in their team. You should definitely have their number and email in your contacts list and you will see them at every board and committee meeting (unless they deputise the latter) that you will ever attend.

- They will also be the custodian of all of your director records.

- They (or their teams) may assist with your travel to board meetings and logistic requests regarding meeting packs; they may provide assistance with board portals and iPads: and may also be the arranger of your directors and officers insurance policy and/or deeds of access, insurance and indemnity.

- They will normally travel with the board and are the minute-takers at all board and committee meetings (unless this is deputised to others in their teams).

- They are the person to advise you on conflicts of interest, shareholdings and your legal duties and obligations as a director, and can also steer you in the direction of either internal or external legal advice.

Their role is dynamic, fast-paced and pressured. The company secretary's is a formidable role and as stated earlier is to be respected and recognised for its contribution to well-governed boards.

14

EDUCATION –
'TIL RESIGNATION DO US PART

THROUGHOUT THIS BOOK, you've heard me bang on about the need to get and stay educated throughout your entire career as a director. It's never going to become any less important or less of an issue, at any time during your entire board career (you can't take annual leave from your directors' duties and so it is with director education).

You have to stay up to date with current issues, changes in the law and best-practice amendments (or contemplations). You need to remain agile in how you work as a director and be open to new developments as they arise across the sphere of company directorship.

I've talked earlier about the importance of getting yourself to a certain baseline (especially in the financial sense), education-wise, before joining your first board. As also stated earlier, plenty of people won't (and just don't) do this. Instead, they leap straight onto a board at their first invitation. It's not illegal to do this – there's no minimum education standard, certificate or course to pass before you can sign a Consent to Act. Your decision to proceed with an appointment will come down to your own personal risk appetite and what you're comfortable with. A lot of people believe that directorship is something that can be learned "on the go". They think "I'll work it out when I get there". True, you will definitely build up your directorship knowledge and education over time, simply by turning up! But the ability to learn on the hop will be deeply influenced by the quality and experience of those you will have with you around the board table. If you are joining a board where your fellow colleagues are not particularly well-versed in directors' duties, are less than financially literate, or have not been exposed to basic risk, strategic or operational competencies, then you may need to give your own educational stock a big re-think.

Also, if you are not somewhat educated or at least have some clue about what it is you are doing, then how do you know whether what's happening on your board is any good? How will you know any different? It just makes sense to get yourself to a minimum foundation point. Even if it's just to get the light to go on and build from there.

The Australian Institute of Company Directors

Your education can start with basic of research on the internet, moving later onto something more substantial and progressive. You can source fantastic starter courses through the AICD (www.companydirectors. com.au) which offers the following tools for members:

- An exceptional and timely director resource centre
- A varied annual events calendar for directors to stay up to date on key matters and to network
- A good selection of director courses (basic, intermediate and advanced – delivered online and in person)
- An annual directors' conference
- An annual essential directors' update which summarises all key

changes in the directorship sphere that have arisen or emerged
during the calendar year

- A monthly journal which includes an excellent variety of articles
  on very topical directorship and business matters.

The AICD can advise you on which course to start with, relative to
your professional and director's experience.

Apart from being a member, I have absolutely zero affiliation with
the AICD and am not paid to promote them in any way. They are the
preeminent organisation for directors and directorship in Australia.
They are also very active in their engagement and lobbying of governments for director and company reforms.

The AICD seeks to develop networks of directors and you can even
find yourself a directorship position via their online portal of
opportunity listings (this is an additional cost to a basic membership
but well worth it to get access to 'live' board vacancies that you may
not otherwise be privy to). They also provide extensive directorship-
related resources and research.

The Governance Institute

The Governance Institute (www.governanceinstitute.com.au) is
another Australian-based organisation which is devoted to the
advancement, study and education of corporate governance (and more
recently risk management education). Membership with the Institute
will provide you with access to educational opportunities, including
tailored courses, governance guides, best-practice publications,
templates, conference options and other learning and development
opportunities.

Membership includes a subscription to their monthly journal
which is extremely insightful regarding contemporary governance
issues and challenges in Australia for directors.

Other director-education providers

Universities also offer educational opportunities in the areas of applied corporate governance, financial governance and ethics and other related areas. Undertaking this type of commitment is extensive and you would need to have a very strong interest in the legal side of governance and directorship to take this step.

Don't underestimate the value in attending annual director conferences, subscribing to newsletters or blogs (as long as the authors are appropriately qualified, e.g. legal firms), networking and chatting to your fellow directors about best-practice and developments in the field. You can also discuss these topics with the company secretary who will have an inherent interest in all things company directorship and governance-related.

I know I go on about education and have done so throughout the entire book, but it is just so very important. It's like any other profession which requires its subjects and participants to be consistently updating their credentials, learnings and competencies to stay at the top of their game.

While there is no one organisation that you must join to be vetted as a director, you really should actively undertake and engage in regular education. Even just reading a monthly director or governance publication and the odd blog is tremendously helpful to building your knowledge-base.

Highly-credentialed directors will engage in a combination of options throughout each year and indeed their careers, recognising that no one element can deliver everything they need to be a competent and contemporary director. This should also be your aim – don't do this half-baked.

Give yourself every chance of being the best version of directorship you can be.

The gift of intuition

There's no denying the importance of education via the written word and experience. But there's also an often over-looked tool lurking in your director's toolbox that needs your attention: it's your intuition.

Plenty of people may denounce the idea that intuition has anything to do with being a great director (that person is typically described as experienced, well-educated and informed, balanced in their views and opinions, and someone who works to the facts in front of them). They are all important qualities, undoubtedly so.

However, from my own personal experience in corporate governance, and from my time working with and observing many dozens of directors over the years, I think there's something quite important to be said about giving some airtime to the soft but persistent whisper that wriggles its way into your brain:

"This doesn't feel right"
"What's wrong with this picture?"
"Why am I uneasy about this?"
"If I don't ask this question will I regret it?"

Don't fight your intuition.

I'm not saying necessarily that you should slavishly follow your intuition and abdicate all decisions to it. However, you will know in your own personal and executive life how often you've heard your intuition telling you something and you've regretted either not acting on it or at least giving it a decent hearing.

Intuition[42] is described as being "…how the mind can 'see' answers to problems or decisions in the absence of explicit reasoning – a 'gut reaction'".

---

[42] www.theconversation.com; accessed 17th November 2014

In my own career I've learned the hard way with intuition. What you wrestle with is the choice of action or inaction that accompanies whatever's awaiting your decision.

Your intuition is an extension of your skill-set. I know too well from experience that if I do or don't do something in a particular way, sure thing it will come back to bite me later. It always does the circle and lands back in my lap. I never get away with it but I always learn from it.

It's a way of saying that if it doesn't feel right or pass the sniff test, then it probably isn't right. If, for example, information is given to the board in haste, or the timing of a decision is being pushed by the presenter (based on perhaps some pretty dodgy or weak business case credentials), or the subject matter rationally lends itself to being deeply researched to bring the decision to a more considered outcome, then in your role as a director you need to pull this up and ask why? If you need more of something or you just need something else entirely, persist with it until you can shake it off.

Test out and deliberate with your intuition. Mull it over; consider the angles; can you overcome the doubts? Or are you just over-thinking what's in front of you?

Your intuition is a very powerful weapon in your professional and personal arsenal. While I'm not advocating that you up-sticks from rational thought and decision-making altogether to give it all over to intuition, if it does come knocking, put the kettle on and invite it in for a cup of tea. See what it has to say. It costs you nothing.

> *The only real valuable thing is intuition.*
> *Albert Einstein*[43]

---

[43] www.brainyquote.com/quotes/quotes/a/alberteins165188.html

AND SO WE REACH THE END

AND SO WE land in the last part of the book – you've dutifully made it this far and it's time for us to wrap this thing up! If you've taken in all parts of this book you'll not be surprised by my parting words as I wish you well on your directorship journey – whether you are ready to start now, or perhaps in a few years' time. Whenever you're ready to go, remember these key elements:

- Keep a copy of *Eyes Wide Open* handy to guide you through the first few appointments you go after. The various checklists (throughout and at the back of the book) provide easy reference to make sure you schedule all the meetings you need to have pre-appointment to any board.

- You owe it to yourself and those who've nominated you to do a thorough due diligence pre-appointment. Keep a clear head and clear mind when considering any opportunity.

- Every person sitting around a board table is a human being who puts their pants on the same way you and I do. Yes, they are to be respected and you will learn amazing things from working alongside them in the boardroom but you must never feel intimidated, over-shadowed or out-classed by them in any way. That thinking is to be banished from any non-confident sector in your brain.

- Building a directorship career takes time (lots of time!), commitment, patience and perseverance. These things aren't built overnight so stay true to your goals and only ever sign up for what you can properly commit to.

- Yes, you do have to earn your stripes on a board with your fellow directors and with the executives (not to mention shareholders and other stakeholders). It takes time and you will definitely make a few mistakes along the way. But you must also recognise that, given the commitment you plan to give to your board career, in time you will absolutely be able to hold your own with your colleagues and gain the respect of your stakeholders.

- Being on a board is not a competition about how quickly you can impress your new stable-mates.

- I always want you to remember that regardless of how senior, well-respected, experienced or highly-esteemed a person is on your board, they have all made mistakes, they all came from a boardroom starting place of zero (just like yourself) and they will not be right on everything – no one can be.

- Take your time to do your research and back yourself to give directorship a go. There are a lot of people out there who get themselves onto a board and then work out later how it all works. Good luck to them, because lucky is what they'll be if they never land themselves in hot water. When has preparation ever been a bad thing in your commercial or professional life?

- Directorship is a serious task, albeit one that should be filled with tremendous learnings and experiences. You have the power, capability and control to make your decision about joining a board that you're comfortable with. Take your time – don't ever feel obliged or pushed into accepting an appointment you're not comfortable with.

Regardless of whether your directorship aspirations are to reach the board seats of an ASX-listed entity, to give your all to a local charity, or to sit on a family board with vast commercial holdings – or anything in between – whatever it becomes, ensure you always uphold the responsibility you owe to society, the institution itself, the shareholders and the stakeholders.

The quality of each of the parts in corporate and not-for-profit Australia is absolutely critical and when directors let the side down it makes it tremendously hard on other spokes in the wheel to do their job well. On the flipside, strong and courageous boards that are committed to their companies and the interests of those attached to them are to be commended and supported.

Enjoy the trip.
Robyn

THANK YOUS

THEY SAY IT takes a village to raise a child; this is also a terribly apt phrase about writing a book!

Bringing a book to life takes many ingredients: it needs the author obviously, but more than that it needs mentors, supporters (your partner, friends, colleagues, etc.), a very patient publisher, endorsers, designers, editors and other reviewers.

So let me acknowledge the following people who have been absolutely instrumental in this special journey:

- My husband Steve – first and foremost for your tremendous patience, support and unwavering confidence in my ability to make this happen; for doing so much more than your fair share in our lives for the past 10 months! Thank you for being in my life – you are the greatest gift I will ever have.

- My publisher Lesley Williams – your patience, flexibility, support, teaching and guidance has been just so wonderful in this process. You took a risk on me and I'll always be grateful. Thank you so very much.

- My book mentor – Nick Barnett. We did it! You gave me the belief I needed to know I could make this book a reality. You've been so generous in reviewing multiple versions and providing your honest feedback and an endorsement. Thank you for that fateful book launch invitation.

- To my other reviewers and endorsers – Peter Wilson, Anne Ward,

Dr Jess Murphy and Michelle Gibbings. I'm thankful for you taking the time and interest in reviewing the book, and for your generous provision of endorsements. You've collectively made the book a better product than I ever could have on my own.

- The Hon. Steve Bracks AC – my sincere thanks for showing your support by writing the Foreword. I'm most grateful.

- To Mark Bland – for your legal review of the book. A most generous gift of personal time and commitment from such a busy human being, to ensure everything was in order! I'm truly indebted – thank you.

- To my many dear and special friends – your ongoing support and encouragement has meant so much to me throughout this journey.

- And finally to my mother Dorothy ("Dottie") who, although no longer with us, is responsible for the drive and determination she has given me to run my own race in life and for instilling in me the importance of working hard and respecting your profession.

GLOSSARY OF TERMS

An online copy of the *Corporations Act 2001* can be found by conducting a name search (under Commonwealth Consolidated Acts) at www.austlii.edu.au.

Aboriginal and Torres Strait Islander corporations. (verbatim from *Corporations Act 2001* – Section190B). This Division (Division 1 – General Duties) does not apply to a corporation that is an Aboriginal and Torres Strait Islander corporation.

Note: Division 265 of the *Corporations (Aboriginal and Torres Strait Islander) Act 2006* deals with the general duties of directors, secretaries, officers and employees of Aboriginal and Torres Strait Islander corporations.

Refer: s190B *Corporations Act*
Division 265 *Corporations (Aboriginal and Torres Strait Islander) Act 2006*

ASIC. Australian Securities and Investments Commission. ASIC is an independent Commonwealth department/body which regulates Australia's corporate, markets and financial services sectors.

Refer: www.asic.gov.au

Company secretary. The company secretary is an 'officer' of the company and is usually referred to as the chief administration officer. Their duties and responsibilities are outlined in the *Corporations Act*. Persons holding this role must sign a Consent to Act form (just as directors do) before commencing their duties. They are also usually considered the chief corporate governance person in the company, and are in charge of ensuring all corporate compliance requirements are satisfied. They provide best-practice recommendations on governance frameworks, processes and systems. The company secretary takes the minutes of all board meetings unless delegated to others. They are appointed and dismissed by the board and usually have an independent direct line of escalation to the chairman.

Refer: s188 and s201D *Corporations Act*, as well as the provisions relating to officers e.g. s180-184

Consent to Act. This is a document which evidences your written agreement to become a director or secretary of a company. Your appointment (finalised) cannot take place or be registered with ASIC before you have completed and returned this form to the company. You should always keep a copy of this signed and dated form for your own personal records.

Refer: s201D *Corporations Act*

Constitution and replaceable rules. A company's constitution is a document which is approved by the shareholders and comprises all of the rules and regulations by which the company is governed, operated and administered. It is one of the key primary documents of the company. If a company does not have a constitution it can use the Replaceable Rules found in the *Corporations Act*. A company can also have a combination of Replaceable Rules and constitutional clauses.

Refer: Table of Replaceable Rules – *Corporations Act* s141
Corporations Act s9 (Constitution)

CSR. Corporate social responsibility. The Australian Centre for Corporate Social Responsibility uses the following truncated International Organization for Standardization definition:

"Social responsibility is the responsibility of an organisation for the impacts of its decisions and activities on society and the environment, through transparent and ethical behaviour…"

"…An authentically Australian approach to CSR integrates strategic approaches with social needs."

Refer: Australian Centre for Corporate Social Responsibility

ESG. The environmental, social and governance considerations that investors consider when investing in companies. More and more investors today are looking to understand how companies are integrating ESG risks and ESG opportunities into their business strategies to create long-term sustainable and responsible businesses.

Greenfield opportunities. These are investment or development opportunities which are not held back or hamstrung by the previous thinking or experience of others.

Group think. This is a situation where the individuals who belong to a group, e.g. a board, conduct their deliberations or decision-making so as to always reach consensus, even if it means that some members concede their own privately-held views. It might be where disruption is not valued or where the group seems intent on doing any one thing or reaching a pre-ordained conclusion.

Group think is often seen as a potential impediment for boards, as it does not encourage a diversity of opinion, thought or debate which in turn can lead to less-informed or less-robust decision-making.

KPIs. Key performance indicators are measures by which people, organisations or departments are measured and held accountable over a specific period of time, regarding pre-agreed/pre-set business or strategic business objectives (measured as outcomes).

Nominations committee. This is a formal sub-committee of the board which is usually constituted to consider the composition, succession-planning and operational effectiveness of the board. The committee may be the primary forum on behalf of the board to oversee the nomination and interviews of new/replacement directors in accordance with the board's nominations policy.

Quorum. This is the minimum number of people who must be present to allow resolutions to be passed at a meeting. You can't pass a resolution without a quorum – the quorum number is written into the company's constitution and the board's charter.

Secretariat. A secretariat – in the context of a board of directors and their company – is the person or group of persons responsible for ensuring that all legal and best practice administrative, compliance and governance requirements are met by the directors and the legal entity. This is also the person or the group who prepares and distributes board meeting packs, drafts; circulates and finalises minutes of meetings; constructs and administers key board policies; or who provides advice to the board on corporate governance developments and best practice. The secretariat naturally includes the company secretary/ies, as well as their support teams or other governance officers.

READY RECKONER
PRE- AND POST-APPOINTMENT
DIRECTORSHIP CHECKLISTS

**One of life's most painful moments comes when
we must admit that we didn't do our homework,
that we are not prepared.**

MERLIN OLSEN[44,45]

The before-anything checklist

☐ Have you even heard of this company before?
☐ Has this company been on the front page of the newspapers?
☐ Can you identify the company's reason for existence
☐ Who are they, what do they do?
☐ Does anything not align with your moral compass and ethics?
☐ Would you be happy to tell anyone you know that this is your board?
☐ Are you still keen?

Board composition checklist

☐ Who is on the board?
☐ Who are the company's executives?
☐ How long have the directors been appointed for?
☐ Check director and executive turnover

---

[44] www.brainyquote.com/quotes/keywords/homework.html; accessed 28th March 2015
[45] http://en.wikipedia.org/wiki/Merlin_Olsen – Merlin Olsen was an American football player, commentator, broadcaster, and actor.

- [ ] Look at the board's diversity (in terms of male/female, geographically, experience and educationally, skills, specialisations, age)
- [ ] How does the diversity sit with you?
- [ ] Are the directors located (geographically) away from the company's head office or main operating locations?
- [ ] Is the board an equal representation model or does it comprise a majority of (or all) independents?
- [ ] If it's a family company, who has been appointed and is the hierarchy apparent – do they have any other external parties on the board outside family?
- [ ] How are directors appointed, by whom and when?
- [ ] What is your feel for the board's composition and size?
- [ ] Start taking notes now to ask questions with the chairman, CEO, CFO, company secretary or other directors.

The opportunity checklist

- [ ] Why has this opportunity come about? What has driven the recruitment?
- [ ] How was the opportunity introduced to you?
- [ ] What's your intuition telling you?

Culture checklist

- [ ] How does the company and the board lead culture on a daily basis?
- [ ] How is culture tested, how often and by whom? Does that seem sufficient to you?
- [ ] What is the staff turnover like?
- [ ] How does the board work together at meetings and outside of the boardroom?
- [ ] What level of respect do the directors show for each other, regardless of their backgrounds or appointment circumstances?

☐ Behaviourally, what's absolutely never tolerated?

☐ Who sets the boundaries of what's an acceptable culture?

Don't be blinded by the financial strength of company to predominantly justify and pre-empt your decision to join this board.

Chairman checklist

☐ You must meet with the chairman in person – at least the very first time

☐ Feel comfortable to ask for more than one meeting if necessary

☐ Explore their history with the company as a director and as chairman

☐ Ask why the opportunity became available

☐ Does the chairman freely discuss culture, strategy and risk – did they unilaterally raise and point to these topics, or was it up to you to do so?

☐ Look for openness, confidence, vision and transparency

☐ Test their thoughts on the CEO and the executives (the CEO is the key)

☐ What does the chairman believe to be the company's greatest strengths, challenges, opportunities and threats?

☐ How do they view the financial viability of the organisation?

☐ How prominently does risk (and risk culture) figure in their discussion with you?

☐ Check attitudes to OH&S systems, processes, culture

☐ Are there any impediments or other issues to you accepting the appointment if you are eventually approved by the board – either on your side or theirs?

☐ Are there any conflicts of interest you feel you should declare?

☐ As a person how does the chairman strike you?

☐ Does this person display strong leadership characteristics?

CEO checklist

(remember context…company size, type of industry, etc.)

- [ ] How does the CEO articulate the company's values?
- [ ] Explore the CEO's take on culture
- [ ] How do they see the company's strategy for the next 6 to 12 months, 3, 5 and 10 years?
- [ ] What are the top five challenges and opportunities for the company (or the corporate group) – short and longer term?
- [ ] Have them describe the company's risk management capabilities and risk culture – how are these areas resourced?
- [ ] Can the CEO discuss the company's risk appetite and what is it influenced by, how often is it reviewed by the board?
- [ ] Have them describe the executives and senior management
- [ ] How does the CEO view the financial position of the company or group? What do they see as the company's challenges regarding financial sustainability?
- [ ] How would the CEO describe the company's attitude to corporate governance?
- [ ] Where is the company at with IT, social media and digital (strategies and capabilities)?
- [ ] Are there any major litigations, government or regulatory reviews underway, anticipated or with the potential to arise in the coming 12 months? If yes, are these standard and recurring reviews or is the review or litigation arising linked to a particular past event?
- [ ] How well does management interact with the board?
- [ ] What is the company's approach or commitment to CSR (corporate social responsibility) and ESG (environment, social, governance)?
- [ ] Check attitudes to OH&S systems, processes, culture
- [ ] Who is this person? What motivates them?
- [ ] As a CEO, what keeps them awake at night?

Post appointment with the CEO

- ☐ What are the CEO's preferences for contact or communication from you between board meetings?
- ☐ What are the protocols to follow should you need some information on a particular company matter or if you need to visit the company's office?

CFO checklist

- ☐ Can you read and understand the financials? If not, is it because of their complexity and volume, or is it because your financial literacy doesn't allow you to?
- ☐ Financial ratios – how do these appear? Are there any overt trends for you to be aware of?
- ☐ Understand what are the relevant ratios for this industry and business
- ☐ Check and read the Notes to the Accounts and question anything not understood
- ☐ Request information on how and when the company pays PAYG and other taxes
- ☐ Check on superannuation for employees – are payments up to date? Who has responsibility for making these payments?
- ☐ Are there any outstanding taxes?
- ☐ Are there any signs of cashflow or balance sheet insolvency?
- ☐ Are you comfortable with how the accounts are structured? Do you understand the cashflows and how the debt is structured/repaid?
- ☐ As a CFO, what keeps them awake at night?

Meeting other directors

- ☐ Meet at least one or two current (or just resigned/retired) directors as part of your due diligence

☐ Ask about cultural attributes of the company and the board and other matters that may have come up in your meetings with the CEO and chairman

☐ Test the company's commitment towards occupational health and safety and corporate governance

☐ Test their thoughts on the financials, past or future financial performance, other major risks/issues/insights

☐ If currently appointed, are these directors people you can see yourself spending many hours with, and with whom you'll be happy or prepared to stand side by side in the trenches of this boardroom?

IT checklist

☐ What is happening technology-wise in the company?

☐ What are its current IT capabilities (human and otherwise)?

☐ Are there major works programs underway or planned?

☐ How far down the list is technology (and this includes digital capabilities) as a strategic priority?

☐ Is there a board committee that oversees IT development and major projects?

☐ Is there a chief technology officer or equivalent?

☐ Are any of the directors technology experts or highly skilled in this area?

☐ Do the company's IT projects typically run on time and on budget?

Checklist on risk

☐ How does the company embed risk culture into the organisation?

☐ Are risk culture and risk systems valued assets of the company?

☐ How is risk defined?

☐ Does the company have a clearly-articulated risk appetite?

☐ How is risk appetite set (so by whom)? How often is it reviewed?

☐ What are the capabilities of the risk function?

☐ Does the risk capability, infrastructure and investment (in people, training and systems) fit with what you'd expect in an organisation of its type and size?

☐ When were the risk systems and capabilities last audited or formally reviewed by the board?

☐ Is there evidence that risk in this company is dynamic, i.e. it's not treated as a static consideration?

Final pre-appointment bits

☐ The corporate structure:

    ☐ Do a company search with ASIC – look for date of incorporation, directors, registered office, shareholder details, appointment and resignation dates and details, charges, etc.

    ☐ Are there any subsidiaries? If yes, what is their role, overlays / interdependencies with the parent – operational or otherwise?

    ☐ Are there any issues or complexities to understand as a result of this construct?

☐ Get a copy of the constitution, board and committee charters

☐ Get a copy of the last three years of board and committee minutes

☐ Check indemnification:

    ☐ Can the company indemnify you from their assets?

    ☐ If not, get a copy of the D&O insurance policy

    ☐ If the policy is not sufficient, should you be taking out your own private cover?

    ☐ Can you obtain your own independent advice on the policies offered?

    ☐ Consult your risk appetite here – are you generally comfortable, all things being considered, to proceed with what's on offer with or without the insurance?

☐ Deeds of access, insurance and indemnity
    ☐ Is one offered?
    ☐ Does the company offer independent legal advice on the deeds? If yes, take it!
    ☐ Check the provisions relating to access, insurance and indemnification

☐ Board calendars (left to run until approved for the coming year) – check what months and dates are left to run, and raise any liability of non-attendance quickly with the chair and company secretary.

Post-appointment

Board induction

☐ Do you get an induction before your first board meeting?
☐ If not, when does it come?
☐ Who will do the induction?
☐ Is there pre-reading to complete?

Company secretary

☐ Conflicts of interest – what are the company's policies on conflicts, definitions of conflicts and what type of items must be declared (including timings and notification procedures)?
☐ What are the rules regarding joining the meeting by means other than in person, missing meetings, submitting proxies or appointing an alternate for a meeting, taking leave from the board, etc.?
☐ Are there any tenure provisions to be aware of?
☐ What would you constitute a breach of the company's fit and proper policy?
☐ Have the company secretary explain the director review process – timing, personnel, feedback, outcomes, etc.

☐ Are there any other personal disclosure obligations?

☐ If they were unavailable in your earlier due diligence steps, can you now obtain a copy of the board's minutes?

☐ Are there annual director training requirements to be met to remain on the board?

☐ By what format do the directors receive their meeting packs – how far in advance of each meeting are the packs received? Is there a board portal to connected with or do the papers come in hard copy?

☐ Is there a board paper document retention and security policy you need to be aware of?

☐ What are the expectations around directors attending external company events, e.g. launches or shows?

☐ What is the company's policy on directors commenting about the entity, the board or having media contact generally?

Board committees

☐ If being appointed to a board committee, ensure you get a diary date with the committee chair to go through the committee's role, responsibilities, charter, history, composition and any other issues of relevance to your appointment

☐ Obtain a copy of the committee's charter

☐ Meet with the executives who support the committee to understand it more thoroughly

☐ Obtain a copy of the minutes of meetings from the prior three years

☐ Will an appointment require re-training or additional training, either as a one-off or on an ongoing basis?

☐ Check the committee's meeting calendar for the residual year

☐ How does the committee report to the board?

☐ Who is its governance adviser?

Pre-first meeting checklist

- [ ] Arrange an induction (with the executives and committee chairs – but always the company secretary)
- [ ] Review the board calendars (first or recurring) – engage with the process
- [ ] Work out a system or approach to how you will read your meeting packs
- [ ] Know how the meeting packs are sent out to directors
- [ ] Review how and where you will safely and securely store your meeting packs
- [ ] Read your first meeting pack – then Google the Centro case
- [ ] Read the minutes in your first meeting pack – then Google the James Hardie case
- [ ] Always read your board papers (all of them) in sufficient time prior to the meetings
- [ ] Make sure you understand the company's conflicts of interest framework
- [ ] Ensure you are informed about major litigations or regulatory reviews/enforceable undertakings, etc.
- [ ] Ensure you understand the rules about board attendance, codes of conduct, fit and proper behaviour, how alternate directors are appointed
- [ ] Board committees – get along to observe yours (pre-committee appointment) and one each of everyone else's!

INDEX

The author can be contacted at
robyn.l.weatherley@gmail.com